Walking The Cards

A Unique Drawing Method

by

Timothy Michaels

Second Edition

Table of Contents

Preface

Some people have asked where the Angle Transfer Method comes from. The answer is that it's a response to an artist's desire to create accurate, realistic drawings.

Anyone who has ever worked on a drawing or painting and later realized that there was an error on the initial drawing knows how frustrating it can be. The further along an artist is in developing the art, the harder it is to make corrections.

After I spent increasing amounts of time painting, I demanded that my initial drawings be correct in order to avoid these problems later. I developed methods of comparing relationships of objects and features in my initial drawing to be sure they were correct before I began painting. These "checks" evolved from various popular techniques, often used in drawing from life, but they're adapted to drawing from a flat image. As the techniques were developed, I found I could check my drawing even before drawing it. The method of checking became the method of drawing. And, the method could be used for any type of two-dimensional art.

The Angle Transfer Method isn't just for experienced artists to improve their work. It's also a tool for any aspiring artist to achieve an accurate drawing before advancing to the painting or coloring stage.

Accurate drawing is only one part of creating realistic art, but it's an obstacle for many people. Once overcome, creating art can be very rewarding. A good initial drawing makes coloring much more enjoyable.

Introduction

Have you ever tried drawing a portrait of someone and had the face just not come out right? It's probably because the eyes, nose, or mouth were not positioned correctly. The method explained here can eliminate those issues.

This book describes my method of accurately transferring an image of any size to a drawing paper of any size. There's no math or measuring involved and any shape may be recreated with as much accuracy as the precision of the user.

For purposes of learning this method, you will need just three "tools": a sharp pencil, and two postcards. You may use just about any rectangular cards such as greeting cards, picture postcards, or even business cards. I suggest picture postcards only because they are a good size, good thickness, and are rigid.

There are other tools you can use once you have mastered the technique. Read the section on other drawing tools for more information.

The basic concept of mapping or transferring an angle simply involves sliding one card against the other, sometimes alternating them to reach the next point. I refer to this as "walking" the cards.

Although it may sound confusing, once you understand the concept, the process is simple and produces a drawing as accurate and detailed as you choose to make it.

It is highly recommended that you read the first 2 chapters through to the end before starting. This will give you an idea of what's involved. As you read, try to follow the process in your mind.

1 – Overview of the Method

This drawing method is based on transferring a line, at its original angle, from a reference image to the drawing paper. It is used in combination with a set of rules that will allow you to build an image from these angles.

Transferring angles can also be used for checking the accuracy of an existing drawing. Refer to the Chapter titled "Accuracy of Existing Drawings".

We'll begin by transferring a few angled lines, then create a complete drawing entirely of angled lines.

Below is a simple house with a chimney. It has various angled lines connecting all the points.

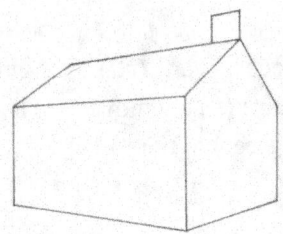

There are several options you could use to transfer the angles of any of the connecting visible or imaginary lines:

1) Use a protractor. You would need to find a reference line and measure the angle with the protractor. Then, go to where you want to re-create that angle and use the protractor to measure there and mark where the new line goes. Complicated, and slow.

2) Use a ruler or straight edge. Just lay a straight edge on the original line, then drag the straight edge to the new

location and you're done. Much simpler. But, you might not place the straight edge at the same angle as the original line. Somewhat inaccurate.

3) Use the Angle Transfer Method. Very accurate and you only need two cards.

Transferring Angles With Cards

In this method, you essentially are using one card as a straight edge, and the other card as a guide to keep the angle intact.

This drawing shows a line being transferred with the card edge lined up at the same angle.

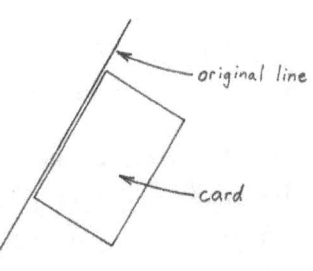

If you were to try moving the card to a new location without changing its angle, you would find it difficult to do so.

So we use a second card (#2) as a guide to keep the angle correct while the first card (#1) is moved. The #2 card is positioned perpendicular (at 90 degrees) to the #1 card.

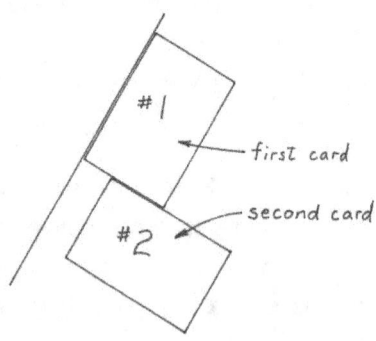

2

If you hold the #2 card firmly in place, you can now slide the #1 card along the edge of the #2 card, while still keeping the correct angle.

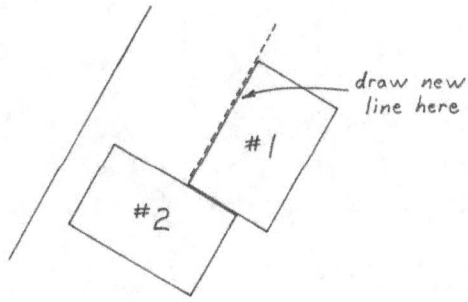

You have now transferred the first line, at the same angle, to a new location.

If you wish to transfer that original line farther away, you simply hold the #1 card in place, and slide the #2 card along its edge.

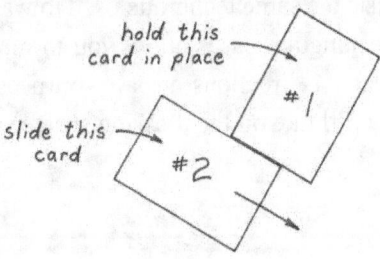

Once you've slid the #2 card as far as you can without losing the angle, it's time to switch cards again.

This time you hold the #2 card in place and slide the #1 card toward the destination at the correct angle.

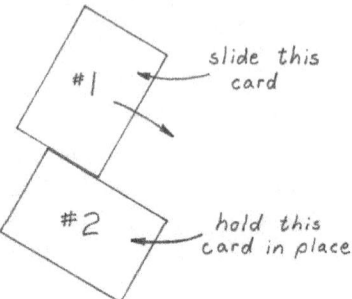

Repeat the process until you have the #1 card at or near the desired location.

Changing Directions

So far you've been able to move a line parallel to itself in two directions. What if you need that line to be moved other directions?

You may position the guide card on another side of the angle carrying card and use the same technique used to walk the cards in the new direction. Rectangular cards allow you to move the cards in 4 directions. But these 4 directions are all you need to zig zag your way to anywhere you'd like on the drawing surface.

And, as long as your cards are rectangular, they have parallel edges. That means you can use either edge to draw your new line.

4

Walking the Cards

This process of sliding the cards and switching their location is referred to as "walking" the cards. It takes some practice, but once mastered, it gets faster and easier, and is very accurate.

With this method you can accurately transfer a line, with its original angle, to a new location. By transferring lines we can intersect them to locate points and build pictures.

Once this method is mastered, images with curves can also be rendered. Even people's faces can be accurately reproduced. If you take the time to learn it correctly you will be impressed with the art that you can create.

Both the maneuvering of the cards and the application of the rules are basically simple. However, they can involve complex strategies which allow for faster drawing and highly accurate and complicated pictures.

To see some art that was created using this method take a quick look at the chapter titled "Art Examples" in the back of this book. Here you will see the original photo, the construction drawing that was created using this method, and the final piece of art after detail, color, and shading were added.

2 - Starting Your First Drawing

To begin you will need a reference image (subject) that you wish to draw which has only straight lines. That image can be a photograph, a picture from a magazine, a greeting card, or any other image. Since you are just learning, it would be best to start with a simple image.

For purposes of demonstration, I will use the same house that was used in the first chapter. However, I have numbered each corner to make it easier to follow the instructions. If your image is a building similar to the sample image, you may number it in a similar manner.

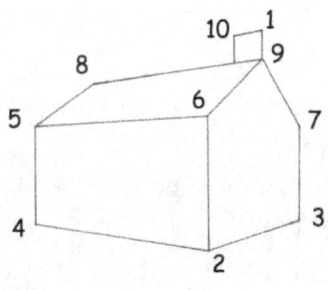

NOTE: If you prefer, you may download a PDF image of this house at: www.TMSartgallery.com

Locating Reference Points

The process of mapping an image begins with a point and a line. On your reference image, identify the highest point, or another significant and reliable point. This point should be easy to identify, easy to remember, and clear (not blurry or vague).

In the example, the chimney is the highest point. A point (dot) is placed on the drawing paper at the upper right to approximately position the chimney's top right corner.

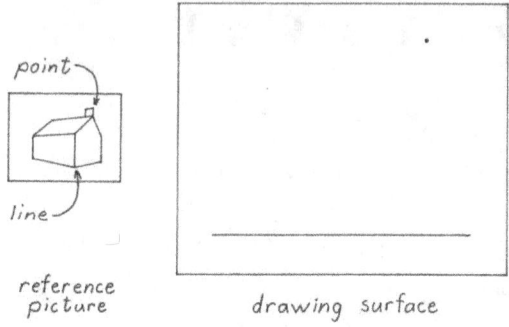

point

line

reference
picture

drawing surface

Next, a point at the bottom of your reference image is selected. In the above example, one bottom corner of the house is the lowest point in the image. To represent this point, a line is drawn on the drawing paper to show how far the house will extend in that direction.

The point (dot) positions the house on the paper, and the line location marks how large the final drawing will be. This sets the scale.

The location of the point and line should be chosen by how easily they can place the subject on the drawing paper with assurance that the completed drawing will fall where you want it.

TIP: It's often a good idea before placing your first point and line to lay pieces of paper around your reference image to help you visualize your desired cropping or placement in the final drawing. This will help you decide where to draw the first point and line on the drawing paper.

If you want to use the whole reference image just the way it is with no cropping, use the upper corner of the image as the point, and another corner of the image for the line.

8

Orienting The Reference Image

The next step is to orient the reference image with the drawing paper and be sure it's oriented the same every time you refer to it. This can be done in multiple ways, but must be reliable and repeatable.

A simple and secure way to do this is to tape the reference image to the top or side edge of the drawing paper. It's best to put the tape on the back side of the reference image and drawing paper to avoid damage to important areas and to keep the tape out of the way. Taping on the front could also cause difficulty when sliding the cards over the surface.

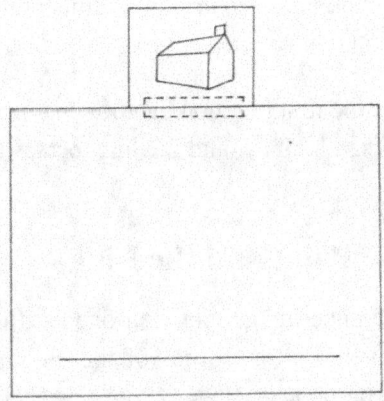

Position the reference image and drawing paper as close together as possible. The less distance needed to slide the cards, the less error you'll have.

A good location for the reference image on landscape oriented paper is above and centered. For portrait oriented paper, a good location is on the side, centered top-to-bottom.

The reference image may be placed anywhere which is convenient, even on top of the drawing paper, as long as it isn't in the way.

TIP: *Before attaching the reference image, you may want to adjust the angle of the photo. If it was taken crooked you should attach it at the correct angle. If the reference image is crooked, your drawing will be crooked.*

For tape, use a low-tack tape if available. If not available, you can reduce the stickiness of regular tape by repeatedly sticking it on the skin, clothes, or table until it's weak enough that it won't damage the drawing paper or the reference image when removed.

Now you're ready to transfer the image. We'll use two cards for this. Postcards, index cards, or photo prints will work, as long as they're not too thin and have crisp edges.

Remember, the first point on the drawing paper represents the top right corner of the chimney, and the line locates the lowest corner of the house.

Connecting the Point and the Line

On the reference image, position one card (A) with its edge crossing directly over the top corner of the chimney (#1) and the bottom corner of the house (#2). Precision here will result in accuracy later.

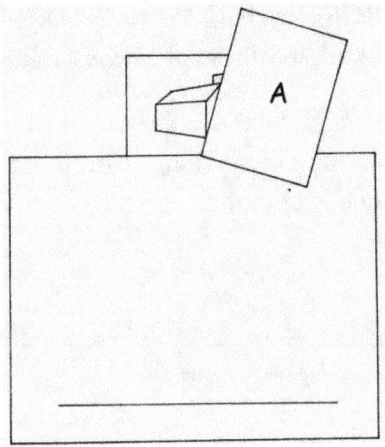

Once card A is aligned as precisely as you can get it, press down on the card and hold it firmly against the drawing paper.

The goal now is to transfer the angle of card A to your initial point and connect that angle with the line at the bottom.

Do this by placing card B against the long edge of card A and slide it down about half way.

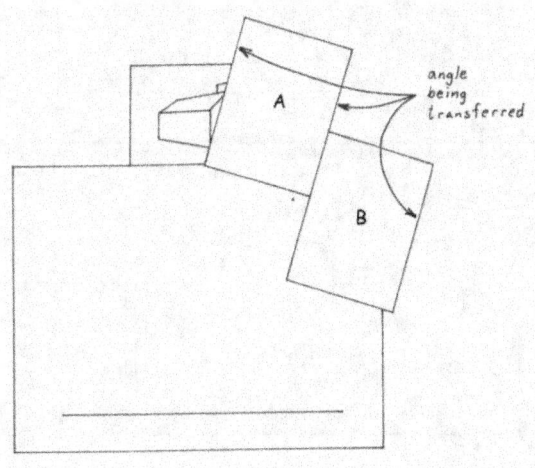

Hold card B firmly against the paper to keep the angle. (We're going to use Card B to carry the angle the rest of the way.)

Then rotate card A 90 degrees and move it to the bottom of card B. The reason for this is to allow card B to be moved closer to the dot while still holding the angle.

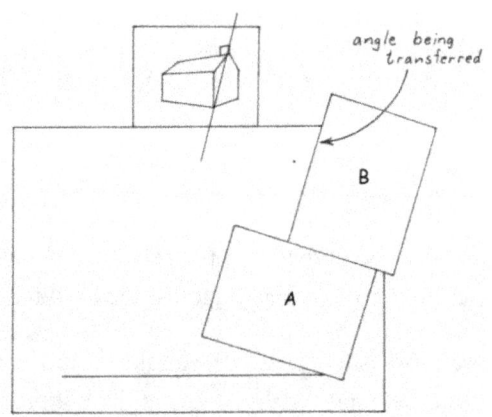

With card B right next to the dot, you can now move card A to the left edge of card B in order to hold the correct transfer angle while you move card B down to the line.

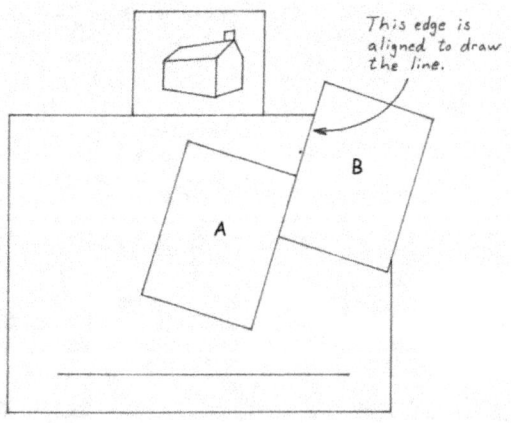

Remember to keep the card that is holding the angle firmly against the drawing paper.

Slide card B down until it crosses the line at the bottom of the drawing paper.

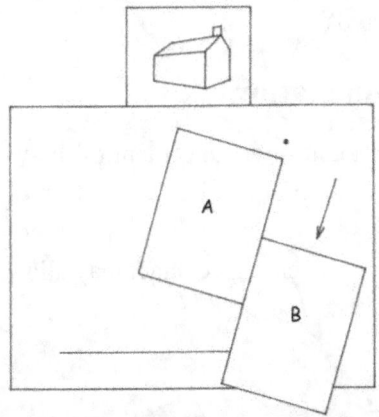

Card B has just transferred the angle and accurately located the bottom corner of the house (point #2).

Lightly draw a short line at the place where Card B intersects the line. That intersecting point is now point #2.

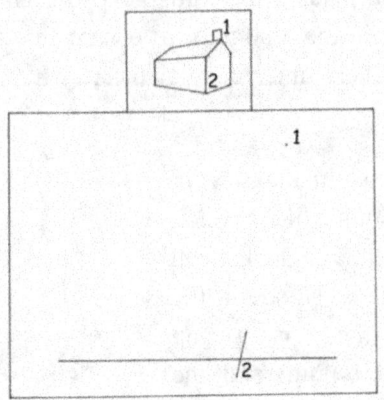

These 2 points, #1 and #2, become the main reference points for locating the other points.

Before proceeding, it is suggested that you go over the card process several more times to ensure that you understand it. Future instructions will not be quite as detailed and assume that you know how to "walk the cards".

Important Information

1.) The amount of advancement of the walked card toward the destination is a compromise between accuracy and speed. Too much contact of the cards with each other will make your advancement slow. Not enough contact may allow the transfer angle to slip.

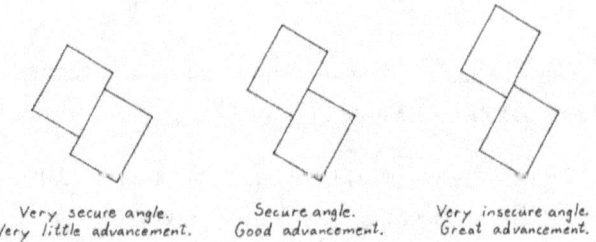

Very secure angle.   Secure angle.   Very insecure angle.
Very little advancement.   Good advancement.   Great advancement.

2.) When placing the cards next to each other, and before walking them, slide them slightly to ensure that their edges are in proper contact. Every time you align a card with another you should check this.

3.) When making your marks, poor positioning of the pencil or card can change the angle that you so carefully aligned. Notice in the illustration that there is a gap between the pencil point and the

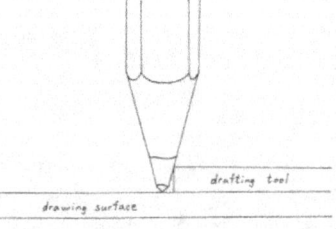

drafting tool

drawing surface

14

card (labeled "drafting tool").

The difference between placing the edge of the card directly over the point and leaving room for the pencil is very slight, but precision is important since this drawing method adds errors together. Small errors along the way accumulate to become significant errors later.

4.) The lines that we will be drawing are construction lines. They should be light and easy to erase.

More Points & Angles

Now that you have the first two reference points, it's time to add other points. These other points will be additional corners of the house in the reference image. Once all of the corners are located, the points can be connected to complete the drawing.

Look at the reference image and find point #3. This is the next reference point we will locate.

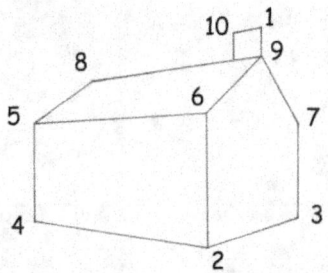

On the reference image (not the drawing) place a card between point #2 and point #3. Now using the cards, transfer that line angle to the drawing paper until the card carrying the angle intersects point #2. Draw a construction line outward from point #2 to the edge of the drawing paper.

15

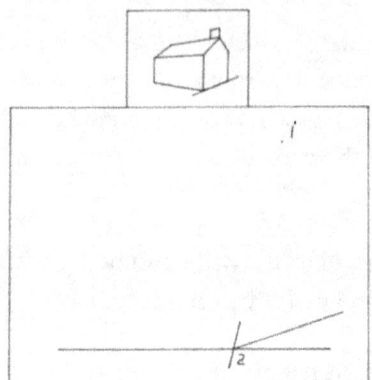

In order to locate where point #3 falls on that construction line, we need to find a line to intersect it.

So let's place a card (on the reference image) between point #1 and point #3.

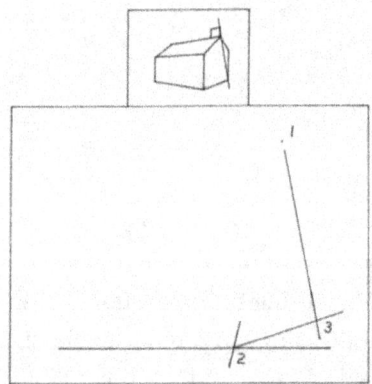

Now walk the cards as needed to transfer that angle over to point #1 on the drawing paper. Where the card carrying the angle intersects with the line outward from point #2, that is the location of our new reference point #3.

We now have 3 reference points that can be used to locate other reference points.

Next we'll locate point #4. On the reference image, position a card between point #2 and point #4. Transfer the angle to the drawing paper until the card carrying the angle intersects with point #2.

Draw a construction line outward from point #2 to the edge of the drawing paper.

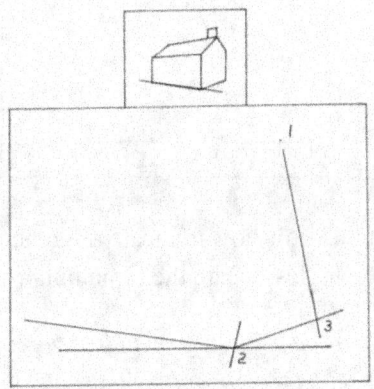

Just like we did previously, we need to locate where point #4 falls on that line.

On the reference image, place a card between point #1 and point #4. Transfer that angle to point #1 on the drawing paper. Where the line intersects with the line outward from point #2 is our new reference point #4.

Now as you draw this intersecting line, it truly represents a line drawn all the way from the initial point at the same angle as is on the reference photo.

We now have 4 good reference points on the drawing. To avoid excess clutter you may want to erase portions of some of the construction lines.

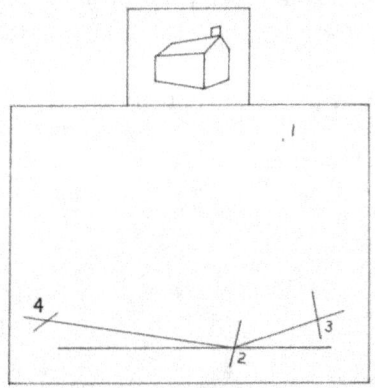

Now that you know how to locate reference points by walking the cards to transfer angles, locate the remaining points on your own.

TIP: *When determining which reference points on the drawing to choose, select the one that will create an intersecting angle on the drawing paper as close to 90 degrees as possible.*

When you have located all of the remaining reference points, erase portions of the construction lines and leave only those portions that intersect with other lines. Then connect the intersecting points on the drawing and your drawing should look like this:

18

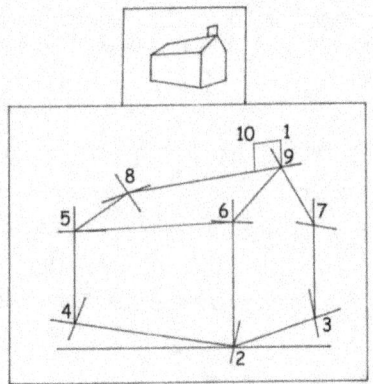

It's not necessary to erase all construction lines if you will be painting and adding shading since they will be covered over.

Errors, and How to Resolve Them

If you transfer an angle from the reference image and it does not line up exactly where it's supposed to, chances are you may have moved the card carrying the angle during the shuffle. Just do it again to confirm that the angle is correct. When holding a card in place, use 2 fingers far apart to avoid having the card rotate.

The other option is to double check the angle by using a different reference point.

3 - Choosing Points to Transfer Angles

After you establish the first two reference points, all others depend on your accuracy in choosing reliable points. Reliable points are usually those that use one of the first two points as a reference, but can also be the points you've referred to most as your picture evolves.

Reliable Points

For example, let's say you created a new reference point (X) using one of the first two reference points. Now you want to create another reference point (Y) using point X. The accuracy of point Y depends on how accurate you were when creating point X. And if you create point Z using point Y, any errors previously will just keep adding to the inaccuracy.

Square

Use the reference point with intersecting angles that are as close to 90 degrees as possible. When angles are too shallow (like 20-30 degrees) or too broad, the chance for error increases.

Errors are additive which can throw off several other points.

Local and Relevant

Use points that are local and relevant.

For example: In the house used previously, the corners of the chimney are irrelevant to the bottom of the house. They are however, relevant to the roof of the house. So when locating those corners, use reference points that are local (close to the chimney) and relevant to their location.

Local points may not be as reliable as some more distant ones, but travelling less distance gives less room for error.

Points relevant to the subject or feature you're drawing may not be the most reliable and may not even be the most local to it, but it's more important that the drawing look right overall with each feature in proper relation to each other than to have accurate placement of a new point you're locating. You need the chimney to be on the top corner of the roof in order to look right, even if you have to move it to get it there. You don't want it floating off to the side even the least bit for the sake of accuracy.

Rules for Walking the Cards

Here are some rules for this drawing method. They apply to the techniques we've already covered and also techniques we haven't yet explored.

1. Always begin with a point and a line. These should typically represent the extremities of your subject.
2. Be sure the reference photo and drawing are properly oriented before each transfer.
3. Slide cards against each other to be sure they're aligned.
4. Use crisp-edged cards or square-edged tools which slide against each other well.
5. Leave room for the pencil when aligning with points on the drawing.
6. Don't slide a card too far to advance a location. Be sure to maintain enough contact with the other card to keep the angle reliable.
7. Choose good reference points for each angle transfer. Consider: Local, Reliable, Relevant, and Square.

4- Curves & Pointless Techniques

You've drawn a house using points and connecting lines. With those techniques, you could build any other image which has only straight lines and corners. But what about objects with curves? Many things in this world are not straight and have no corners.

In this chapter you'll learn a few techniques for drawing shapes with curves.

This apple, next to a block, on a table, has almost no points at first glance. But look again. See if you can find them.

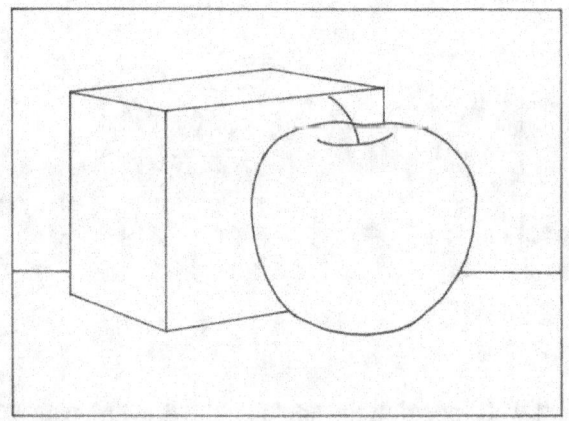

The two ends of the stem may be the first points you see, and the two ends of the dimple. Then where the two edges of the block intersects with the top and side of the apple. Another point is where the back edge of the table intersects the apple.

So, you have 8 possible points to position the apple on the drawing paper. It may not be necessary to use them all.

23

You can photocopy the illustration of the apple and box, or you can download a PDF from www.TMSartgallery.com. Once you have the reference image, tape it to the top center of your drawing paper.

To begin, use the angle transfer techniques from the previous chapters to locate the 6 corners of the box. Start with a point at the top of your drawing paper and a line at the bottom. Now locate the 6 box corners, connect those points and erase the construction lines.

Once again, for purposes of instruction, I've numbered the box corners just for reference. I've also labeled the points that position the apple.

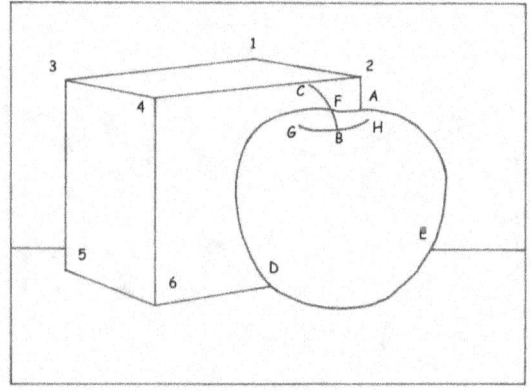

Next we'll position the apple on the drawing paper.

To locate point A on your drawing, use your cards to transfer the angle between point 6 and point A on your reference image to the drawing paper. Draw a light construction line.

Since the box has 90 degree angles, simply draw another construction line from point 2 straight down until it intersects the construction line from point 6 (square, local, relevant). This becomes point A on your drawing. To locate point D, transfer the angle between point 4 and point D. Then transfer the angle from point 6 to point D.

Using this method, locate the points that will position the apple on the drawing paper. Erase the construction lines.

Setting Limits

The next step is to mark each of the points on the apple with a line that provides some direction as to the curvature of the apple's surface. This is done by transferring the curvature of the apple from the reference image to the drawing as it is at each point.

At each point on the reference image that touches the apple, hold your card at an angle that closely matches the surface of the apple. Transfer that angle to the drawing paper. Draw a construction line at that point. When finished, your drawing should look like the following illustration.

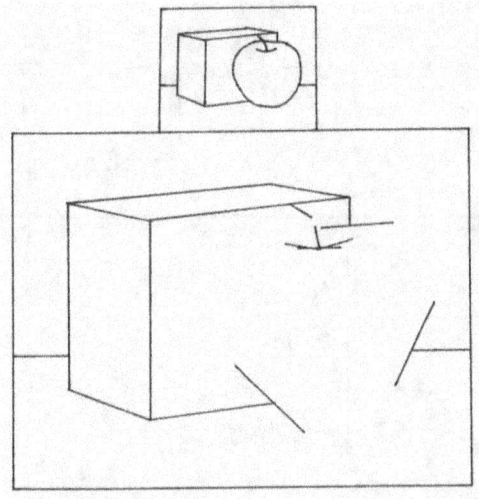

These angled lines will be referred to as "limits". They are not exact points but rather lines that provide a direction and limit for freehand drawing the curved object (apple). Hand drawing the curve involves staying inside the limits and touching, but not crossing each of them.

There are not enough limits in the previous illustration to accurately freehand draw the apple. So we must add more.

Box in the curves of the apple surface further by adding more limits for them. Use the angle relationship between various other points in the reference image and the edges of the apple. To get these angles, position your card on a chosen point and in a way that it touches, but doesn't cross, a surface curve. Then transfer that angle to the drawing paper.

In the next illustration, you can see that some parts of the apple's curve have been represented very well by many limits from reference points. But, other parts of its curves are lacking. If you draw the apple now by hand, you'll have lots of guidance in those

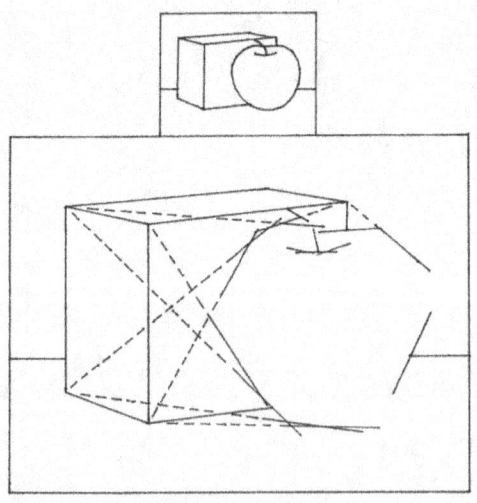

areas with many limits, but less guidance where there are fewer limits.

Since there will be freehand work involved in finishing a drawing with curves, the more limits you have the better. The more limits, the more accurately your curves will match the original.

Sometimes limits may appear to disagree with others due to error. When the limits disagree, you can recheck their angle, or set more limits and follow the ones which agree while disregarding the errors.

Inventing Points

If you want more limit lines to help you define the curve, but don't have reference points to get them from, you may create temporary points to use. These new points may be placed anywhere, but we'll place them in a way to provide the limits we want. In this example they are placed on the reference image. Remember, everything must come from the reference image.

If you're able to draw on the reference image, you may just place "x's" at helpful locations. If you cannot mark on the reference image (glossy print) or don't want to (valuable photo), you may place tape on the reference image and use the corners of the tape as points. You can also put pieces of paper laying partially over the reference or even a piece of tracing paper over the reference in order to draw on it.

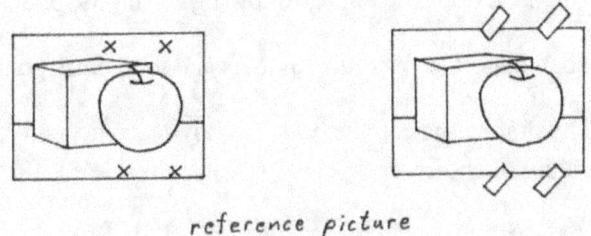

reference picture

27

These strategically placed temporary reference points must, now, be transferred to the drawing, just as you did with all the other points. These points will allow you to create additional limit lines that help draw the shape of the apple. They are local and relevant.

Once you have the temporary points on the drawing to match where they are on the reference photo, you may use them to establish additional limits for the apple. This will continue to box-in the apple curve and increase the accuracy of the freehand drawing of the sides of the apple.

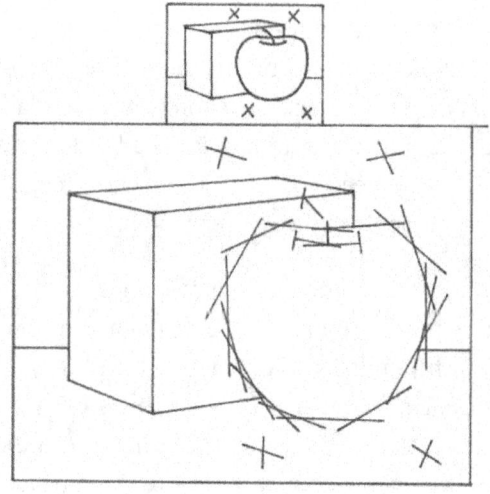

Freehand draw the apple, following the limits for accuracy,

Then erase the construction lines and temporary points.

The drawing is completed and ready to shade, color, or paint in the medium of choice.

5 – Accuracy of Existing Drawings

Now that you know how to carry an angle accurately from anywhere to anywhere else, you can do this to check relationships in a drawing you've already completed no matter what method was used to create it.

This is especially important when doing faces. It is critical that the eyes, nose, and mouth are positioned accurately.

You'll need to place the reference image next to your drawing, oriented the same, and kept secure so it can't move. This means you probably want to tape the photo to the edge of your drawing.

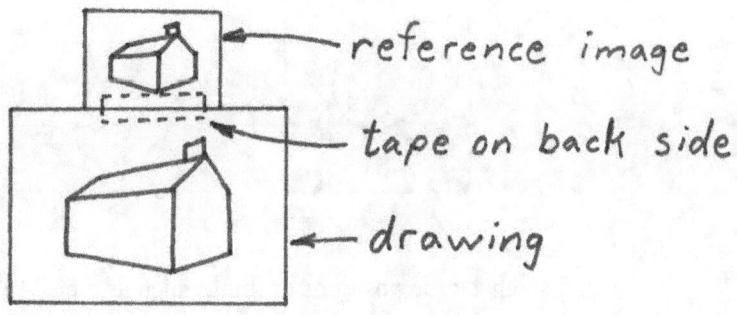

reference image

tape on back side

drawing

Here are just a few things that you can check using the Angle Transfer Method.

You can check to be sure you've drawn your picture accurately by matching the angles of a subject's mouth or eyes on the photo with the mouth or eyes on your drawing. And, also their alignment with each other side-to-side (eyes to nose and mouth).

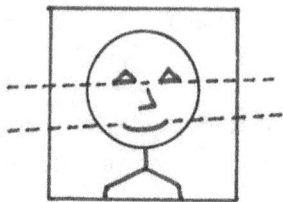

You can check to see that a person's one ear isn't lower than the other. (Or, not any lower than it should be.)

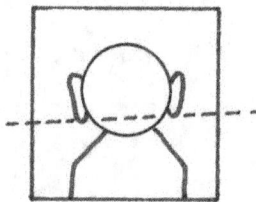

You can also check the positions of things such as a person's head relative to their shoulder.

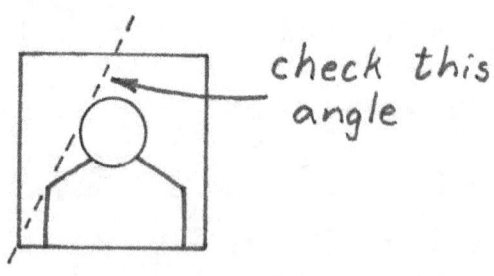

check this angle

Check to be sure your friend isn't any shorter than you (or than they should be).

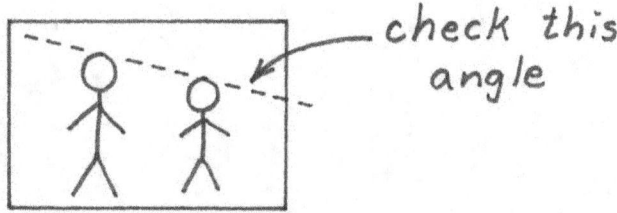

check this angle

Angles of sailboats, leaning ladders, car windshields, or a baseball player's bat.

All relationships between all things in your picture may be checked. Because they're all related by angles.

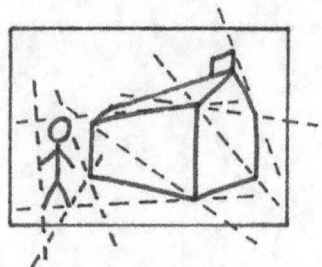

There's almost no end to the checking you could do. Which also means there's almost no end to how far you could go in creating an accurate picture using only angles.

6 – Refining Your Techniques

Locating Vague Areas

Some objects in an image may have vague areas that do not have clean crisp edges. An example would be a shiny area on an apple.

These areas can be represented by roughly boxing them in using various relevant reference points.

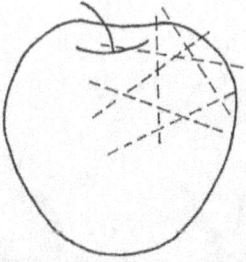

Or, just find its estimated center, then use shading during the finishing process.

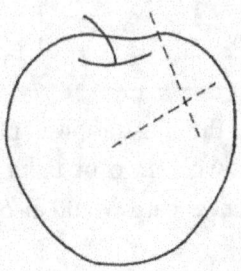

Many vague areas may be located by estimating in this way. Some examples are:

- dark or light areas of cheeks and noses,
- dark and light areas on car fenders,
- light and dark patches of foliage.

Choosing The Right Size Card

One of the cards you use for transferring angles should usually be at least the size of the reference image. This way they can span any two points of the subject.

The card does not have to span the corresponding points on the drawing paper because you can walk from point to point on it while you place the angle.

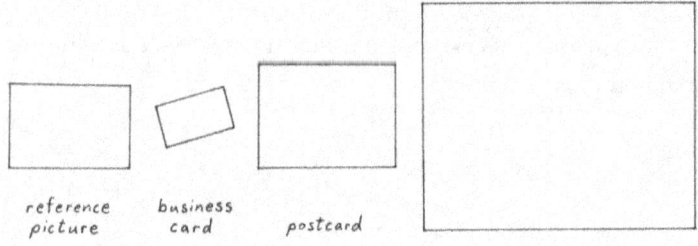

reference picture   business card   postcard

drawing surface

The postcard in the illustration is plenty big enough to span the reference image shown. Two of them may be used, or one in combination with a business card would also work.

The cards should also not be so big that they don't fit well in the drawing space. If they cover too much of the drawing paper, the drawing may become lost and disoriented under it.

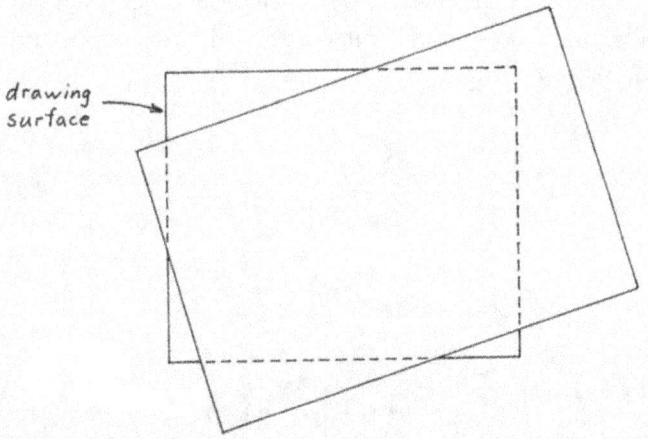

Sometimes the cards are big enough for the reference photo, but too small for a large drawing area (big enlargement). They may require too much walking across the drawing. The more moves you have to make with the cards, the greater the chance of error.

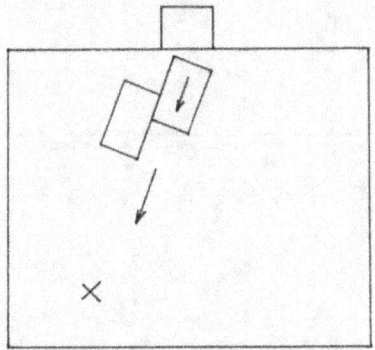

Regardless of the size of the cards used, they will be easier to use if they have parallel edges or perfect 90 degree corners.

A ruler with a square edge may help to quickly and reliably slide greater distances. It is long enough to span distances, but narrow enough not to cover too much of the work space.

However, with rulers, you can only use the long sides to slide. Never align the short sides of a ruler because they don't give sufficient contact at the edge.

Not enough contact area to be sure angle being transferred is correct.

7 - Other Tools for Transferring Angles

Once you have mastered the Angle Transfer Method using cards, you may want to try using other drawing tools as described below. These "tools" need to have good edges and be fairly rigid. Some examples are:

- Book
- Ruler
- Drafting triangle
- Rolling ruler

A rolling ruler has only one straight edge, but can be accurately rolled to easily transfer angles all by itself. An additional ruler or triangle may be helpful for extending construction lines and offer more flexibility with a rolling ruler.

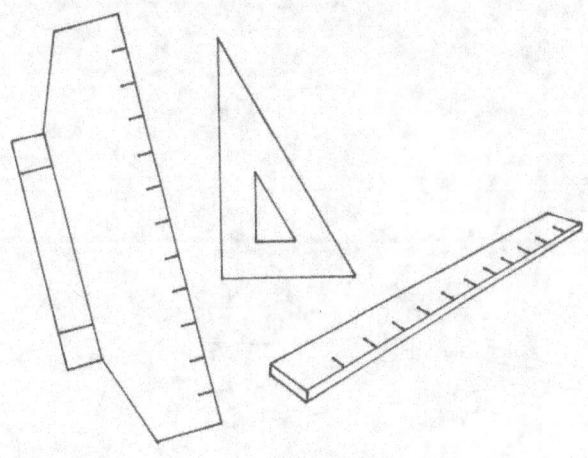

Selecting good tools will affect the quality of the final drawing, as well as the ease with which it is created.

Some triangles and rulers will be good, others not good. A good triangle and ruler would look like this:

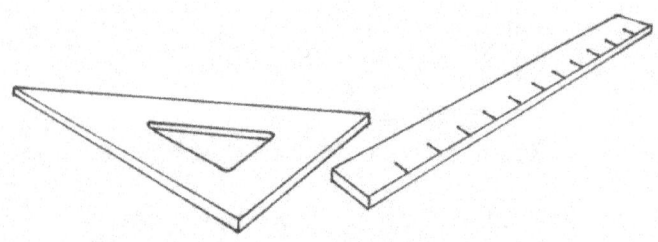

The triangle and ruler below will NOT work well because the sharp edges will easily slip over or under another tool causing you to lose the angle being transferred.

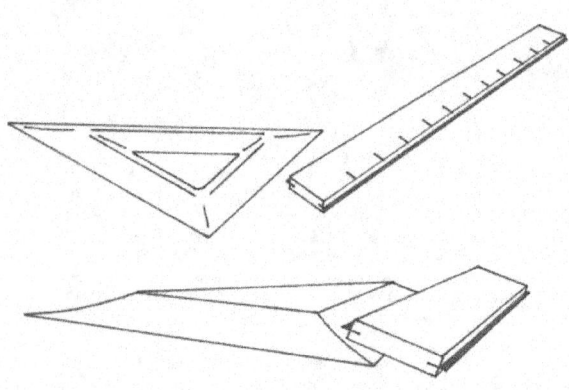

The edges and corners of the tools are very important in order to ensure that you have an easy and accurate transfer. Tool's with at least one 90 degree corner and one straight edge allow you to easily re-orient the tool along the way, while reliably maintaining the angle you're transferring.

Square edged triangles and square edged rulers may also be used successfully in combination with each other, or with a rolling ruler. Being able to manipulate each of them can make your angle transfers much faster and more accurate.

See-thru professional drafting triangles and straight edges work very well for accurate angle transfers. Plus they allow you to see where you're going as you move them.

Using the Rolling Ruler

While accurate and reliable drawings may be done with commonly available tools, like business cards, postcards, and books, a made-for-purpose drafting tool like the rolling ruler can make the work easier and faster.

The rolling ruler is a straight edge ruler with 2 wheels located behind the straight edge. The wheels have ridges to provide traction

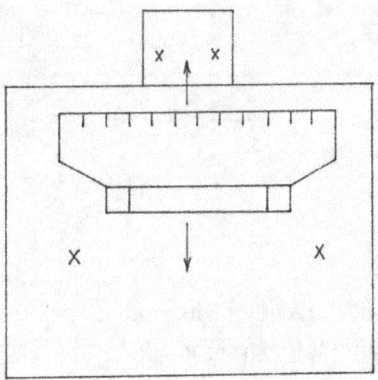

and keep them from slipping. When the straight edge is set to the desired angle, you simply roll it to where you want to transfer the angle. The angle stays constant as it is rolled. When properly used it can be very accurate.

However, the rolling ruler is a little more complicated to use than a plain straight edge.

Proper use is to press down in between the rollers to roll, and then press on the blade (straight edge) to hold its position.

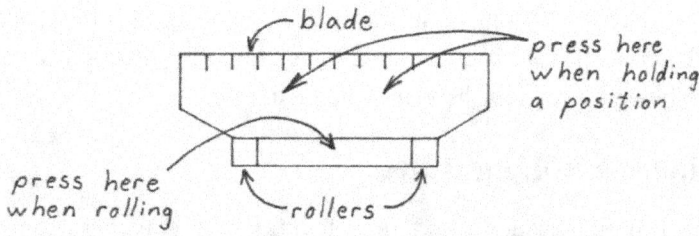

When setting an angle you may either press in two places on the blade, so that the ruler doesn't roll, or press between the wheels and in one place on the blade. Where ever you press, the pressure should be at locations distant from each other to prevent the angle from changing (just as you do with cards).

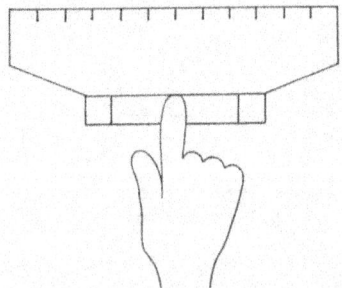

Pressing at the center distributes pressure equally to the rollers and assures you of a straight roll.

40

It also allows the blade to slide gently across the surface.

You must be careful when going over any bumps as you roll to avoid a pivot on one roller, which may change the angle and direction. Bumps may be the edge of a paper, a piece of tape or anything else which may cause the blade to catch.

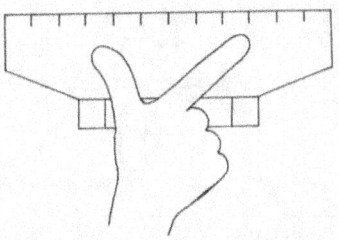

Pressing far apart in two places on the <u>blade as shown above</u>, or on the <u>blade and rollers as shown below</u>, holds it in place to draw a line or use another tool with it.

When holding a position with any tool, always press straight down at two places far apart.

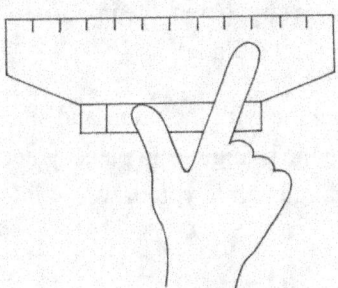

The next illustration shows how you can use a right triangle in combination with a rolling ruler to transfer a vertical line down and to the side, easily.

You begin by placing the triangle in place at the desired angle, and holding it securely against the drawing paper.

Then, you place the rolling ruler under the triangle and hold it in place, releasing the triangle and transferring your fingers to the rolling ruler.

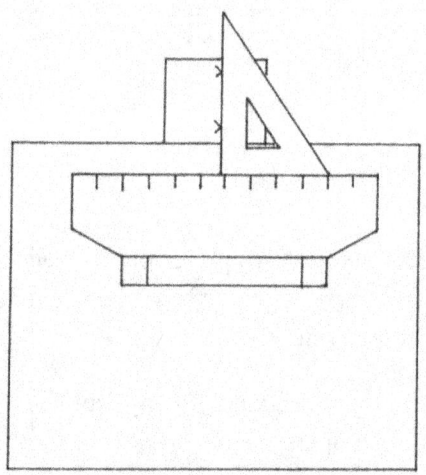

Place your fingers at the rolling position on the ruler and roll it down sufficiently to the target area, then return to the holding position on the ruler (depressing the blade).

Align the triangle with the ruler, and slide it into place where the points are. Once the triangle is in place, you may release the ruler and hold only the triangle while you draw the line.

A postcard may also be combined with the rolling ruler using this same procedure. Just be sure that the edges slide well against each other.

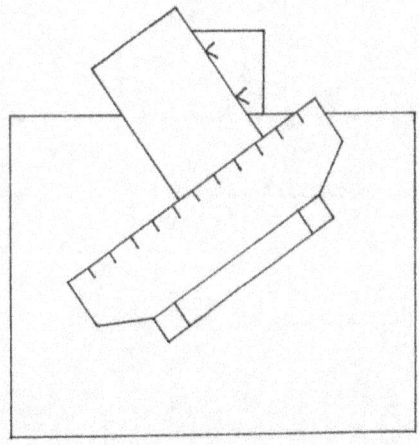

You may find it easier to arrange a triangle and rolling ruler to not roll off the drawing paper than you could with a postcard and rolling ruler.

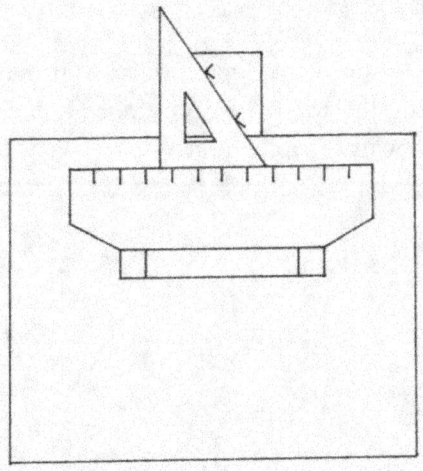

The next illustration shows the transfer of an angle on the left side of the reference image to the left side of the drawing paper.

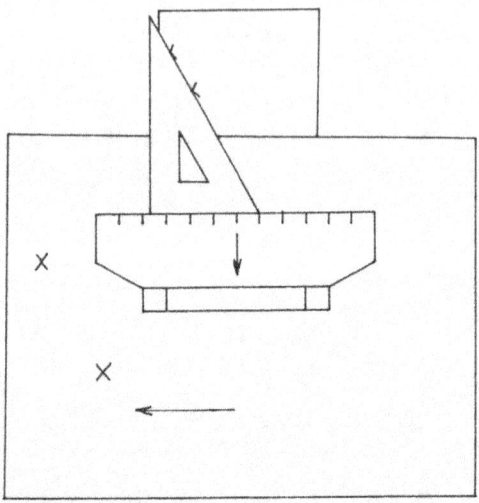

In this example, the rolling ruler is rolled down, then slid to the left against the triangles bottom edge so that it can take the triangle to where it needs to go.

If you run out of rolling surface, you may reposition the rolling ruler along the way. Just remember to hold the triangle in position while moving the rolling ruler.

Here's a different arrangement where the rolling ruler is used to slide the triangle into position.

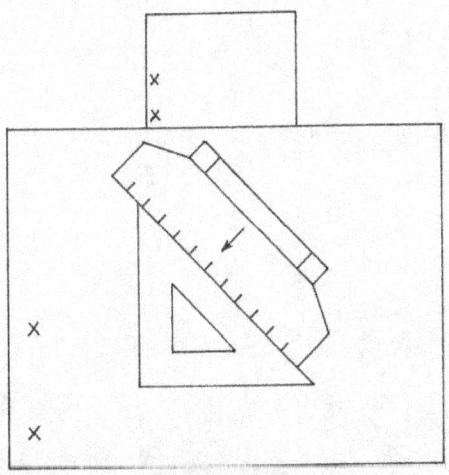

These examples are meant to show how flexible the rolling ruler can be. There is no set way to arranging the tools for a transfer. It's totally up to you. Just keep track of the tool and edge that is carrying the angle.

Using Triangles

Two triangles may also be used together effectively for transferring accurate angles. But, you must be sure to keep track of which one is carrying the correct angle especially if you're making a complicated move. You may want to mark one triangle and always use that one for carrying the angle.

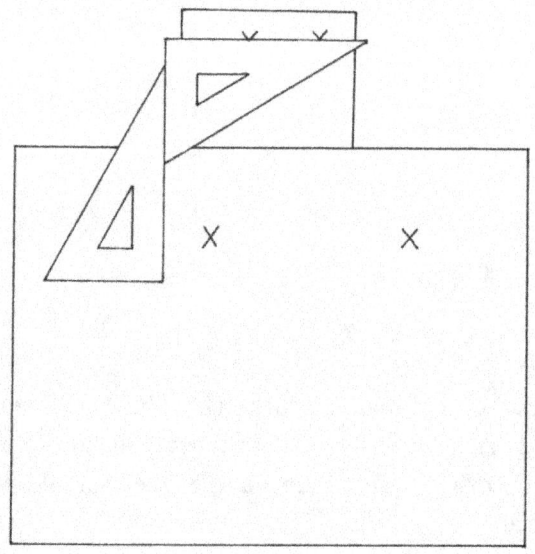

These two triangles may be walked down into place to move this angle.

A note about triangles. Drafting triangles can be purchased as 30-60-90 or 45-45-90. When learning this method, it is recommended that you use two of the same type to avoid confusion as to which side is carrying the angle.

46

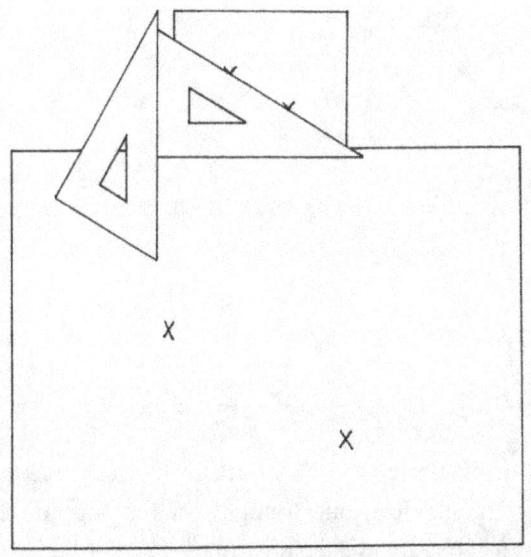

Here is another arrangement of two triangles to transfer an angled line.

If you change the places of the triangles or re-orient them, you must be sure you don't mistake one angle for a different one.

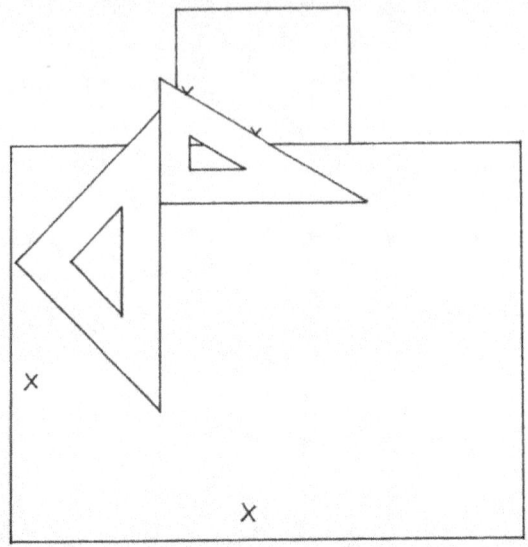

In this example you'll be transferring an angle down and to the left. You could lose one triangle off the edge of the drawing paper as you try to reach the destination.

This procedure gets a bit complicated because your angle transfer "tools" have 3 differently angled sides.

Re-orienting the triangles along the way can get you where you're going as long as you don't confuse which one is carrying the angle.

Once you slide the first angle-carrying triangle down and well onto the drawing paper, you can reposition the second triangle under it for a slide to the left.

48

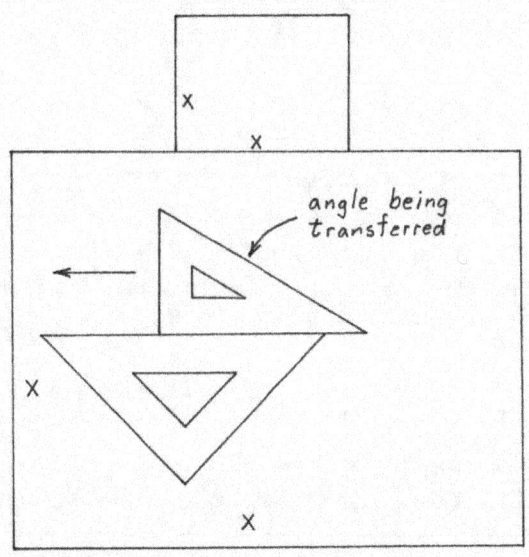

angle being
transferred

Once you're sufficiently slid to the left, you can replace the original angle-carrying triangle with the other one.

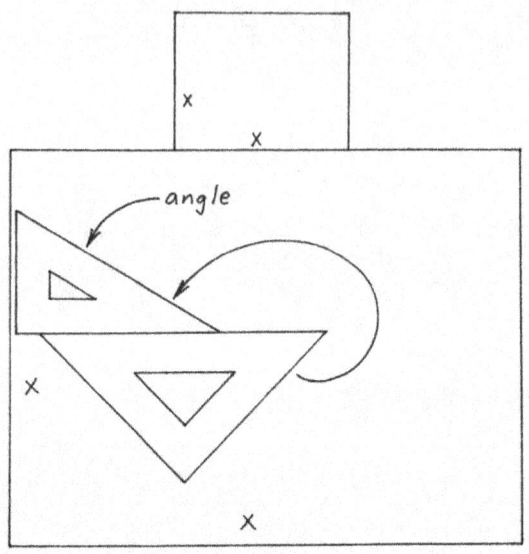

You do this by moving the guide triangle to the upper-right of the angle-carrying triangle and then use it to carry the angle the rest of the way.

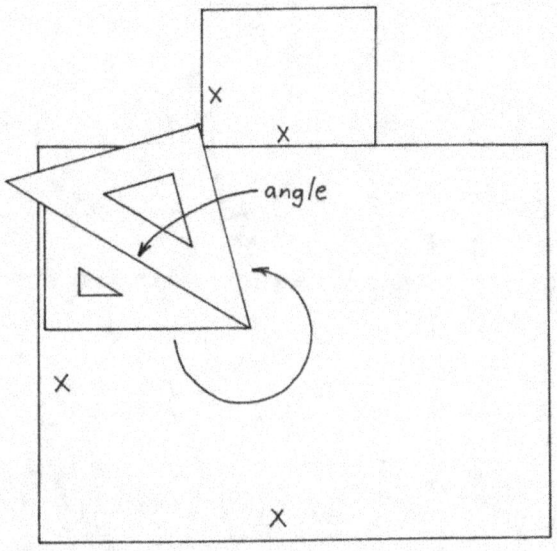

Move the former angle-carrying triangle to the right of the newly assigned one to guide it down and into place.

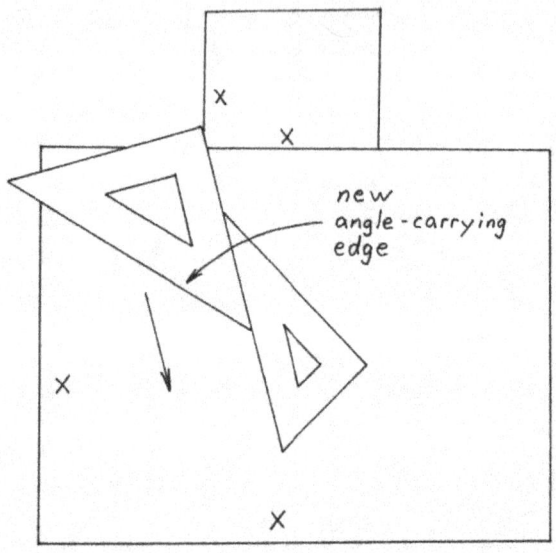

Everything may be repositioned and you may switch the angle carrying triangle with the guide triangle, carefully.

8 - Integrating Other Drawing Methods

The angle transfer drawing method demonstrated uses no measuring. You can scale each of the subjects according to the size of the space you want them to fit into when you're only drawing one subject.

Scaling a Subject

If you know the measurement of how large you want a subject, or part of a subject, or if you know a percentage enlargement or reduction you want, you may apply that adjustment to the placement of the point and line.

The initial line of every drawing sets the scale of the subject. So, the distance from the point may be increased or reduced by a percentage compared to the reference and that percentage scaling will apply to the entire subject. To make the subject a specific measured size, you just need the point and line to represent that part of the subject (or the whole subject) and fix the measurement when you first draw the initial point and line.

This house will be enlarged to 200% (2 times original) because you've fixed the point and line to twice the original.

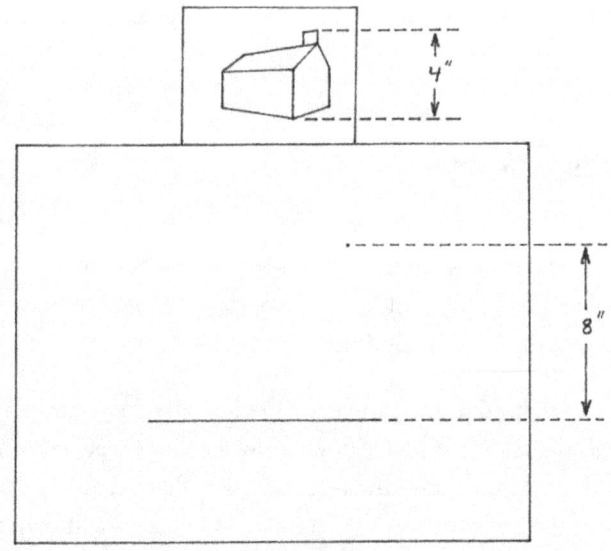

If you've drawn a picture of a house and you want to place a man in the picture, you need to be sure he's sized properly, relative to the house.

A standard house door is 6 feet 8 inches high, so you can use a door to calculate the man's height on the drawing. If you know his height to be 6 feet you may just draw him 9/10 of the height of the drawn door and place him right next to it.

6 feet ÷ 6 feet 8 inches = 72 inches/80 inches = 9/10

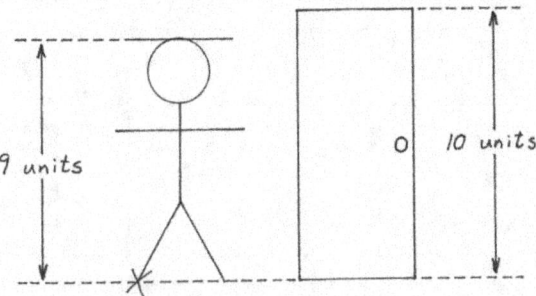

9 units

O | 10 units

To size him for standing next to the door, you use a point and line representing the top of his head and bottom of his feet to place him and begin the drawing of him.

If you don't know his height, you may guess it and then calculate.

If he's not standing next to the door, or at least the same distance from the viewer as the door is from the viewer, you'll first represent his height next to the door, then you'll move him, enlarging or reducing him according to the rules of perspective.

Since you already have the house drawn, you have to size him according to the house. You also have to use the perspective of the house in order to reposition and resize him as he's moved away from the door.

55

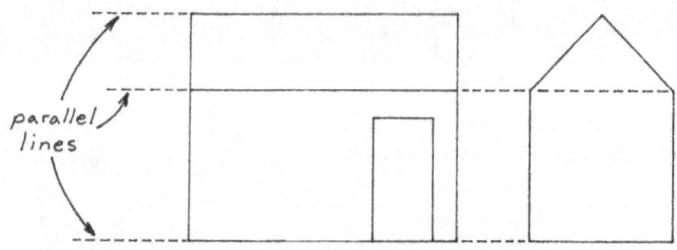

You first find the vanishing points of the house by extending its lines which would be parallel to the ground in a front or side view.

In the drawing below, it looks like this.

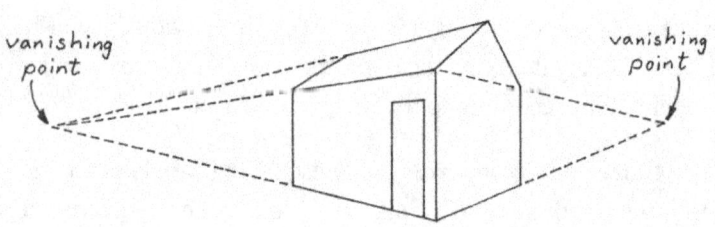

Where these, otherwise parallel lines converge are called vanishing points.

This means that if the house were extremely wide and extremely deep, the far corners would be so far away, they would be so small they would appear to vanish.

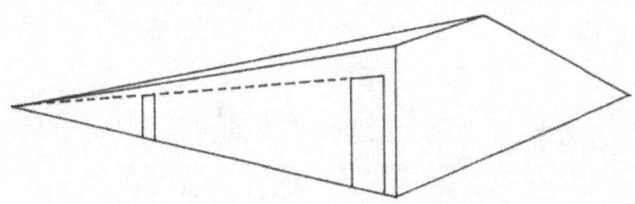

The door would do this also, if it were located further back along the house. And, so would the man.

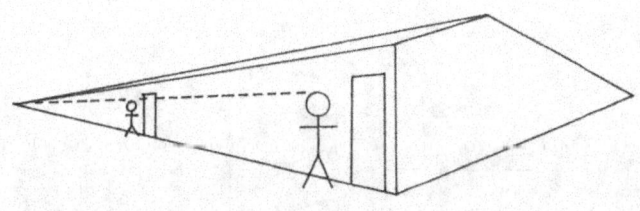

Using perspective helps to adjust his size for how far away he is, regardless of where he is in the picture.

Once you size him for distance, you draw horizontal lines representing the bottom of his feet and top of his head and you may move him left or right along these lines. He remains equally far away as long as he's drawn to fit between these lines.

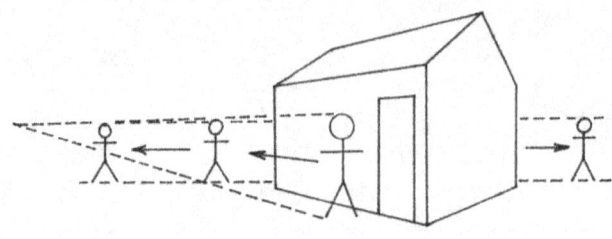

You may use the same method to bring him closer to you. The same lines of the house may be brought forward to enlarge him.

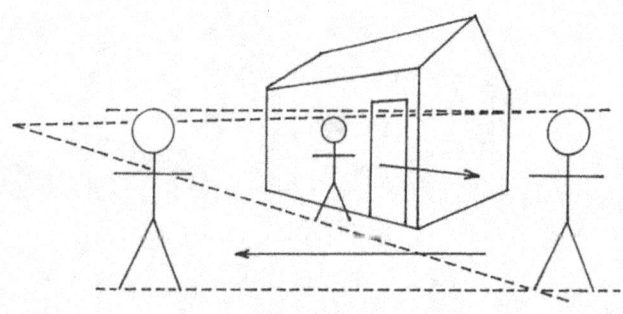

And, now that he's closer, you may move him left or right, keeping his same height and also same elevation from the bottom of the page.

His size tells us how close he is to us. His elevation tells us what he's standing on. So far, you've kept him standing on the same level ground the house is on. If you place him higher or lower than where the house perspective tells us, then he's no longer standing at the same level as the house. He may be up or down a hill.

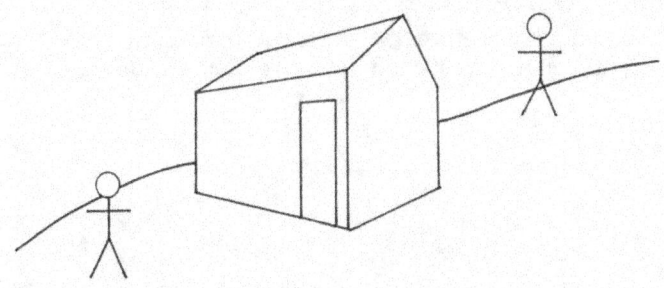

Or, he may be standing in a hole or on a ladder.

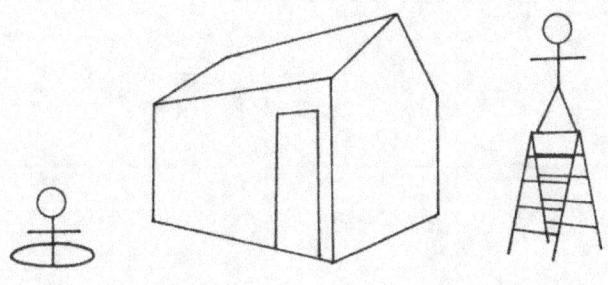

As artists, you have to explain differences in elevation to the viewers.

For most purposes, though, you need to keep him at the same elevation, between the lines.

If, for some reason, the man is already sized and you need to put him in the picture as he is, then you draw the perspective lines to see where he fits (how high up the page he needs to be to stand on the same level ground as the house).

And, you may move him left or right across the page.

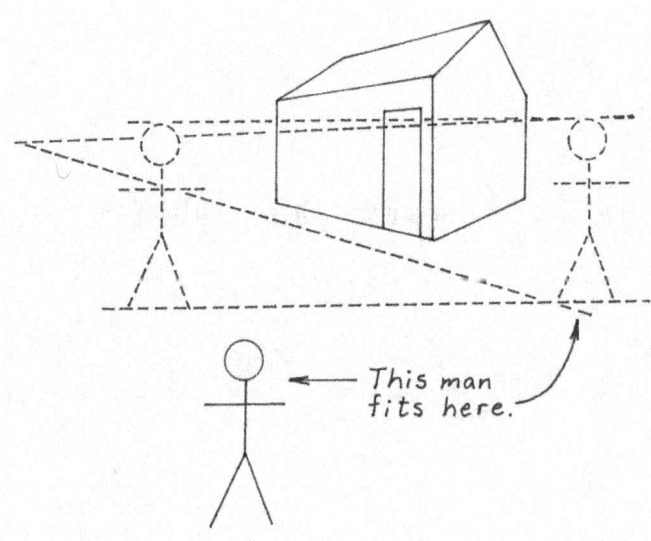

This man fits here.

Viewing Angle

So far, you've assumed that the two images you're combining are being viewed from the same elevation. Before combining any two images, you must first determine their viewing elevation. Mismatched viewing elevations can look very wrong.

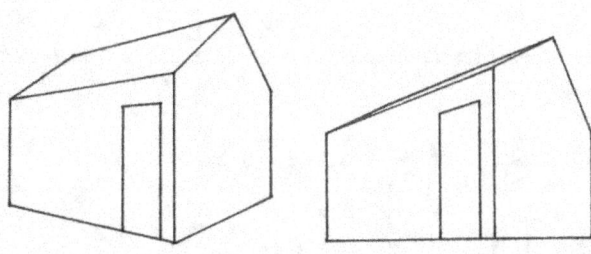

You match viewing elevation by using the same horizon line for both subjects. The horizon line must be found in each image. Then, each image must be drawn using a common horizon line. To do this, you find the horizon line of the first drawn subject and use it to place the other subjects.

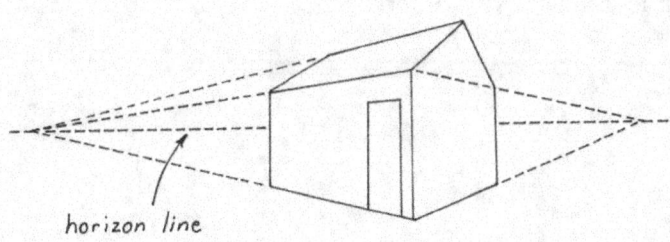

horizon line

Vanishing points tell us where the horizon line is. A line drawn from one vanishing point to another is the horizon line. This line represents the eye-level of the viewer.

Because exact viewing elevations of people can sometimes be difficult to determine, you should use the table next to this man to help.

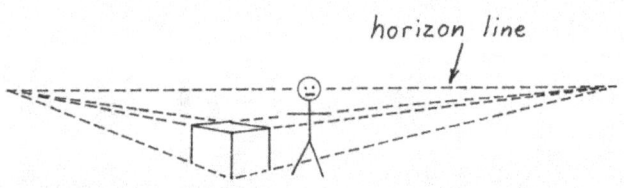

Without the table, you may have to guess. Often, you do have to guess, or estimate, eye level of the viewer.

To combine these two pictures realistically, you <u>must </u>use the same eye level (horizon line). If you don't, one of them won't be upright, as with the two mismatched houses you saw. One would appear to lean backward or forward.

The two houses, and the man, combined, would properly look like this. One house ends up being on a hill.

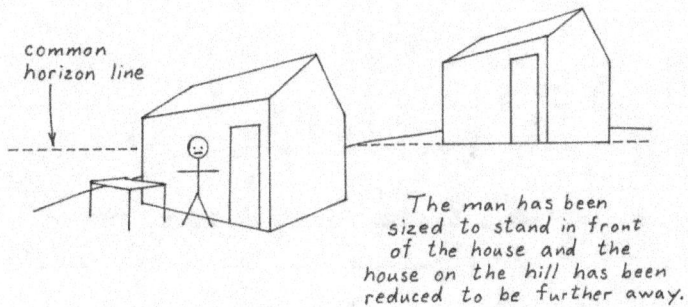

common
horizon line

The man has been sized to stand in front of the house and the house on the hill has been reduced to be further away.

You normally would choose not to combine images with viewing angles which don't agree. But, if you do, you have to find a way to explain their relationship And, if you can't explain why something appears to be leaning forward or backward, then you have to use a common horizon line.

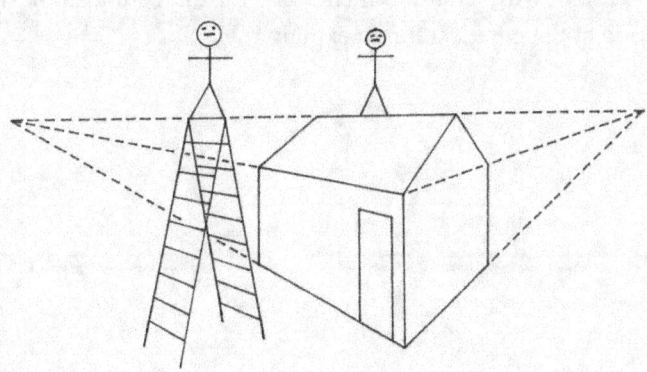

A man may need to stand on a ladder or on top of his house in order to explain why you're looking up at him and down at his house.

63

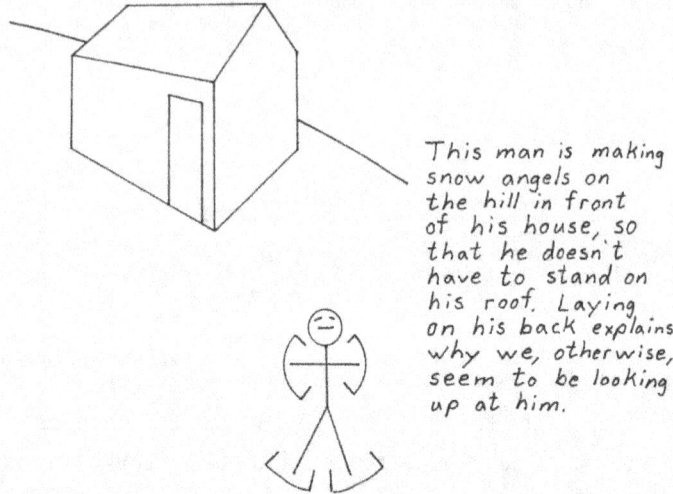

This man is making snow angels on the hill in front of his house, so that he doesn't have to stand on his roof. Laying on his back explains why we, otherwise, seem to be looking up at him.

The best solution to viewing angle issues is usually to choose images with viewing angles which work for the composition, rather than to adjust the composition to explain them.

Parallel Lines

Parallel lines on a subject are often expected to be parallel. Viewers will notice if one is crooked on a geometric-type object, like siding on a house or rungs on a ladder.

When the lines are parallel in the picture, making them parallel in the drawing is easy, you just copy the same angle to each of them.

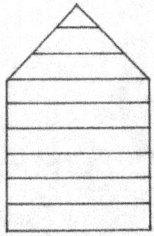

But, if you're viewing the subject at an angle other than straight-on, the lines converge, due to perspective. So, the vanishing point needs to be found and all the would-be parallel lines need to be drawn so that they converge at that same point.

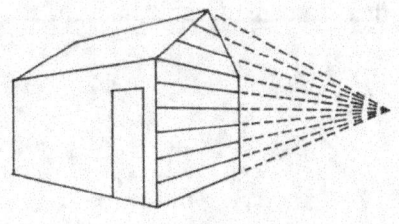

Dividing An Area

Sometimes you may want to divide an area, equally, without having to locate each division. When there are many equal divisions, the variations with transferring angles and locating points could become obvious.

Uneven divisions of something like siding on a house can really stand out to the viewer.

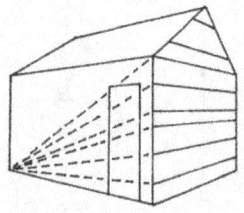

In this drawing, you located the lines of the siding in relation to the bottom left corner of the house. You found where they intersect the front edge of the house and drew them toward the vanishing point. But, errors in locating them on the front edge of the house has caused them to be noticeably uneven.

Since viewers expect to see siding perfectly spaced, you may do better to divide the edge of the house with a ruler.

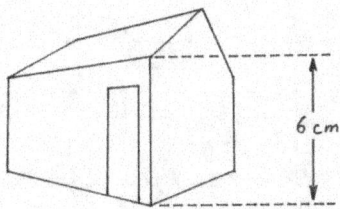

If you need to place 6 boards of siding along the side of the house and one of its edges measures exactly 6 cm, or 6 quarters of an inch, or 6 of any other easy unit, then that's great. If not, you can make the ruler fit. You just extend parallel lines for the space you want to divide, then angle the ruler until you find some unit which you can use to fit 6 of in that area. You mark the divisions and extend them back to the edge of the house.

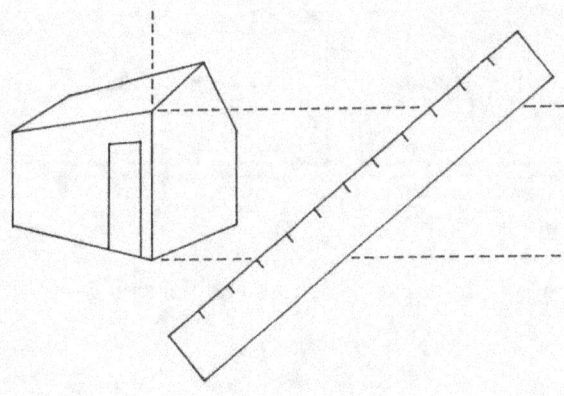

67

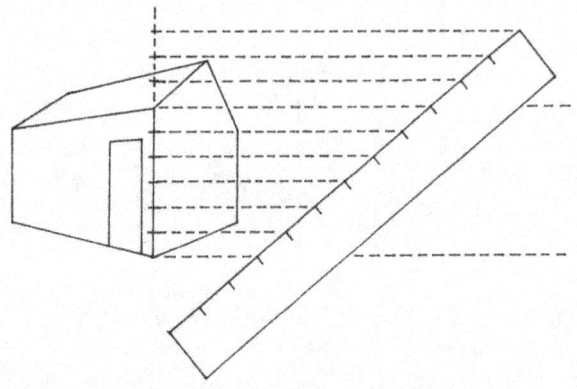

Remember to draw these to the vanishing point.

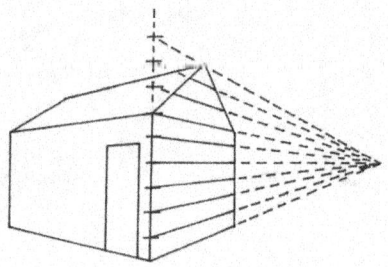

Now, you have evenly spaced parallel siding on the house.

9 - Art Examples

Following are examples of art that was created using this method of drawing.

Each example shows:

First - The original photograph.

Second - A construction sketch created using this method.

Third - The final art piece with details and shading.

Although everything is shown in monochrome, the final artwork could have been done in color using any medium.

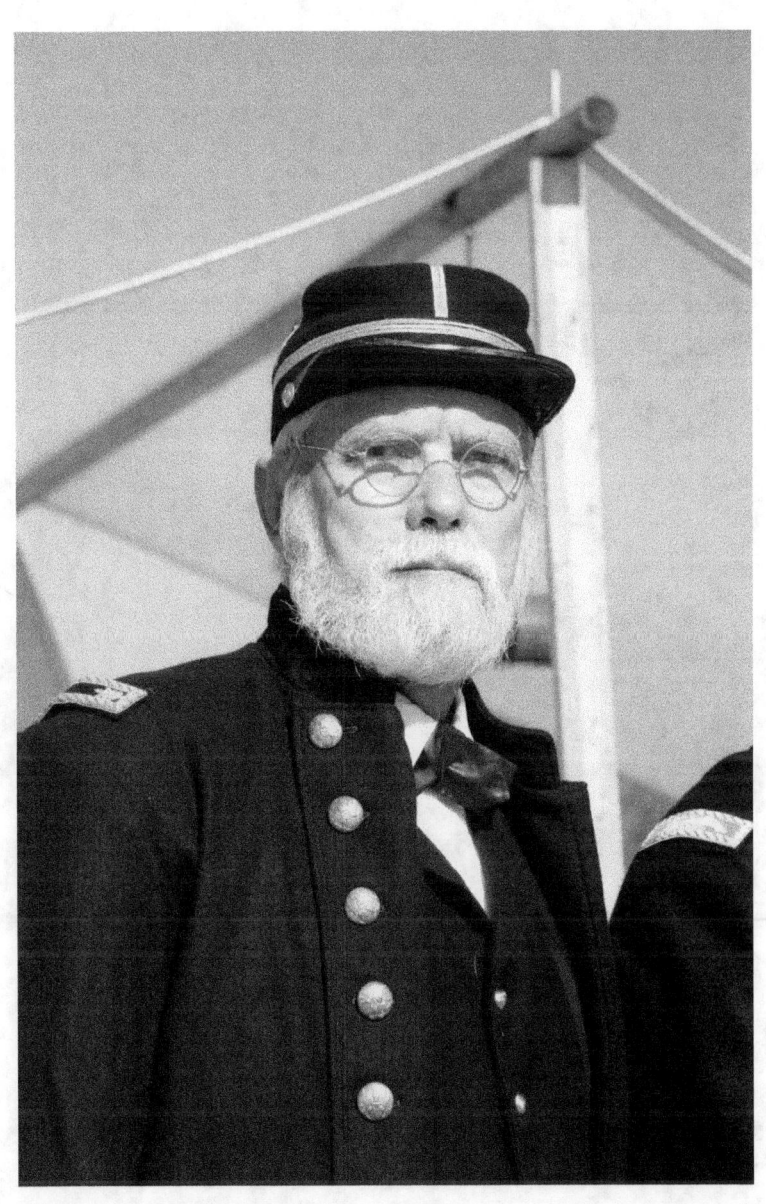

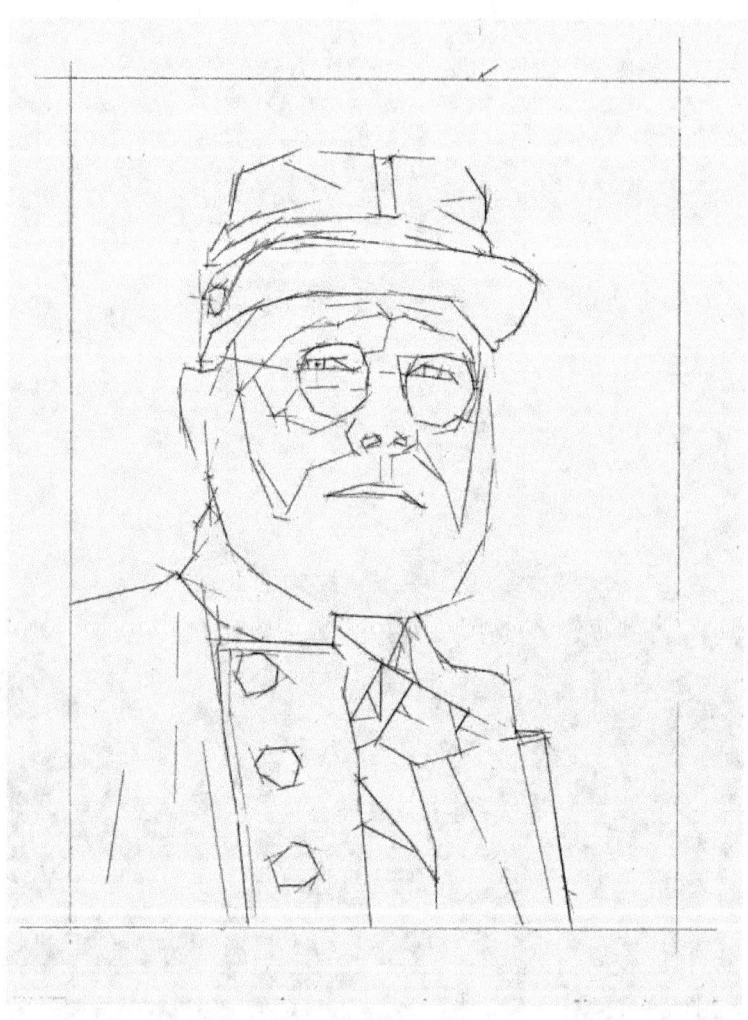

72

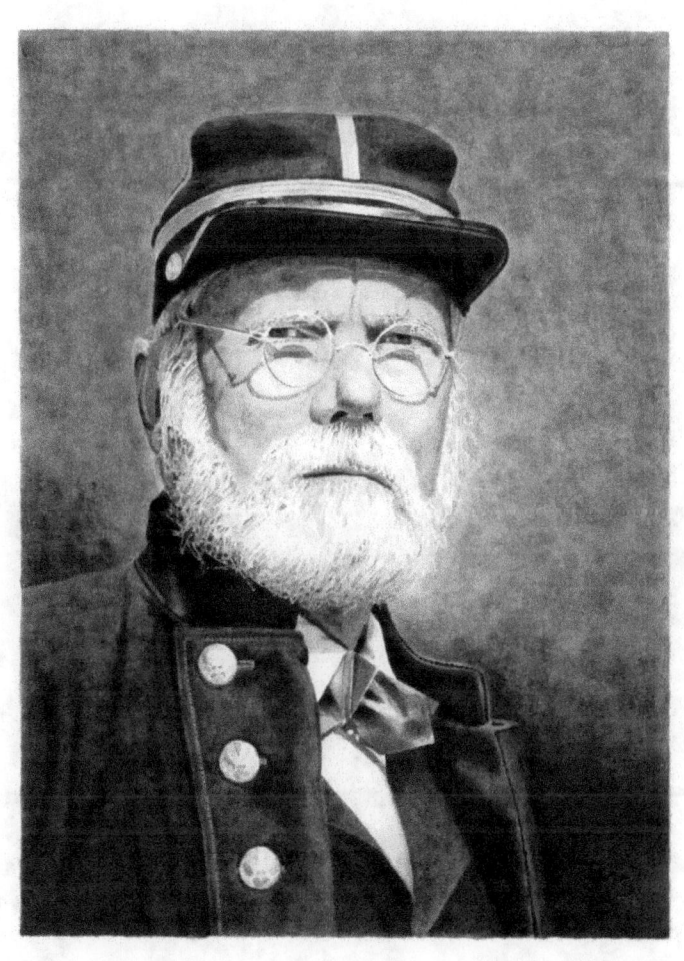

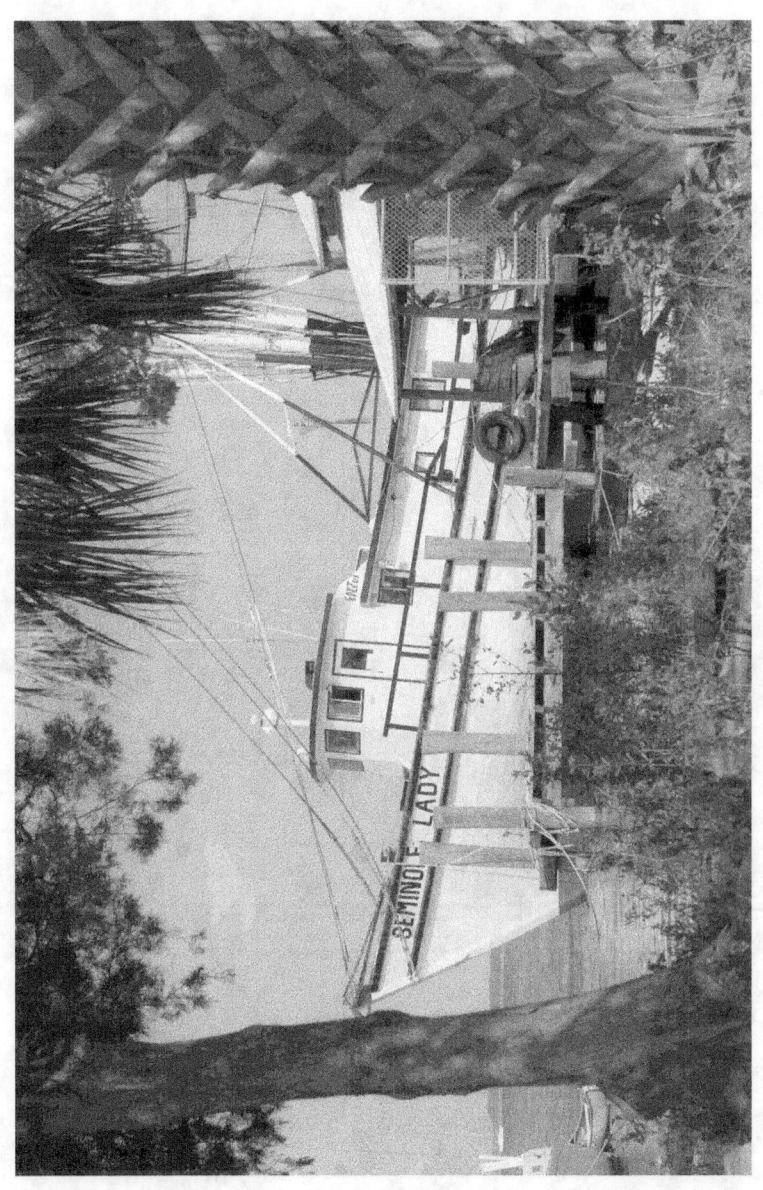

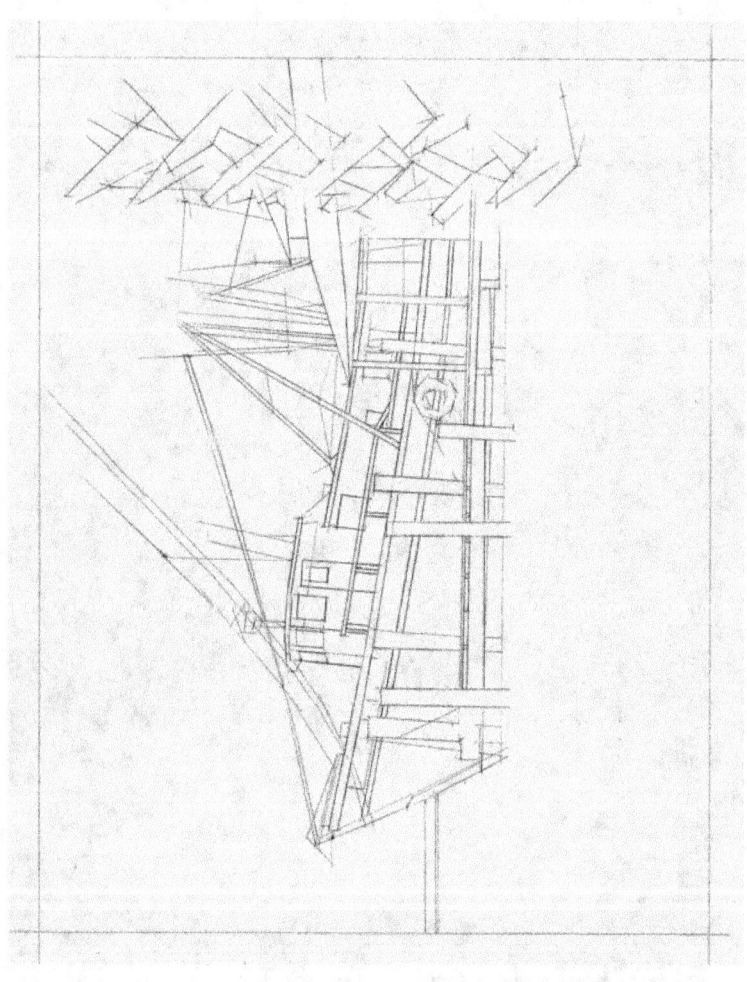

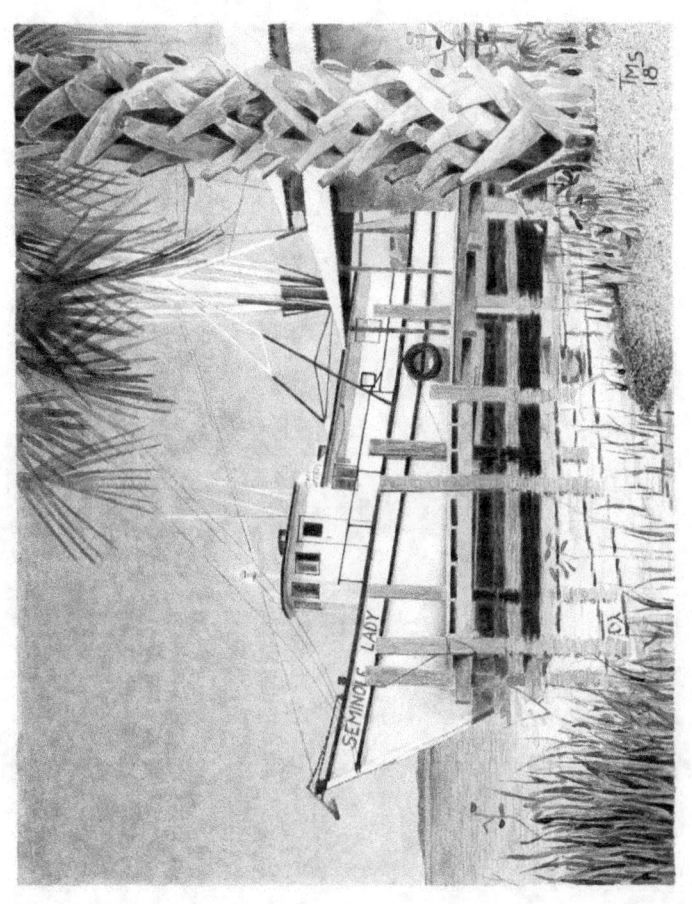

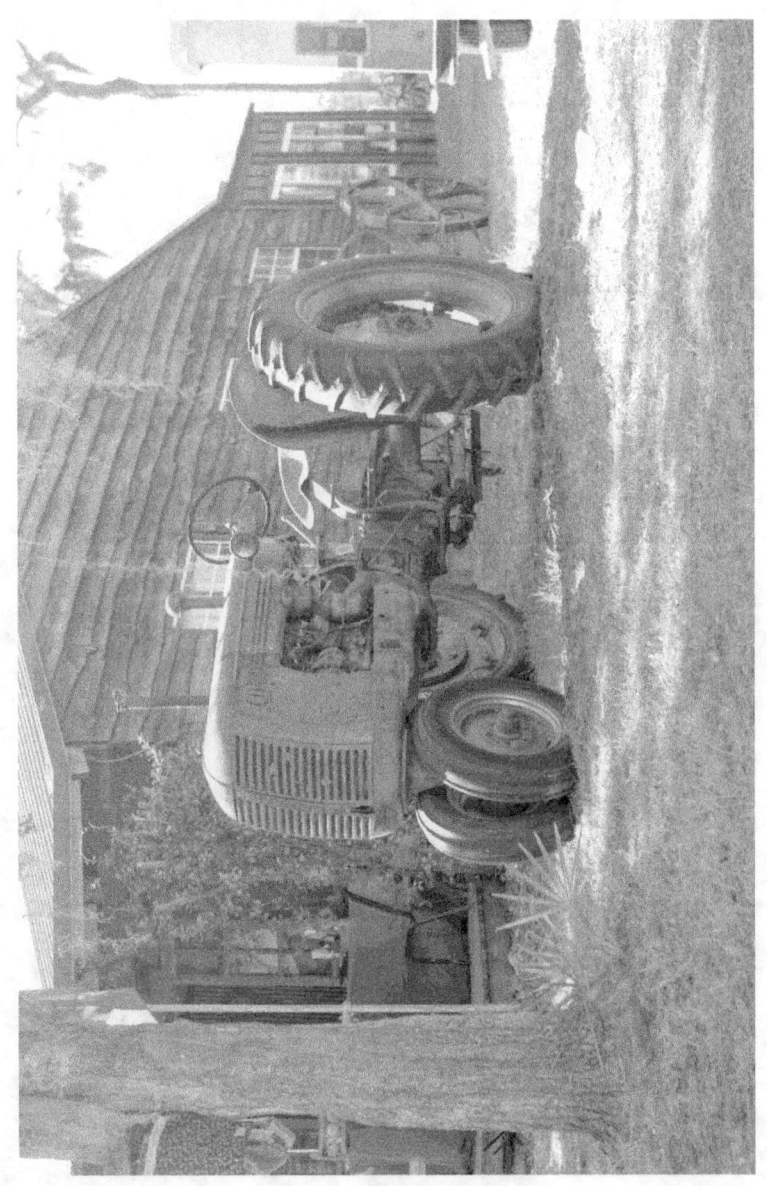

79

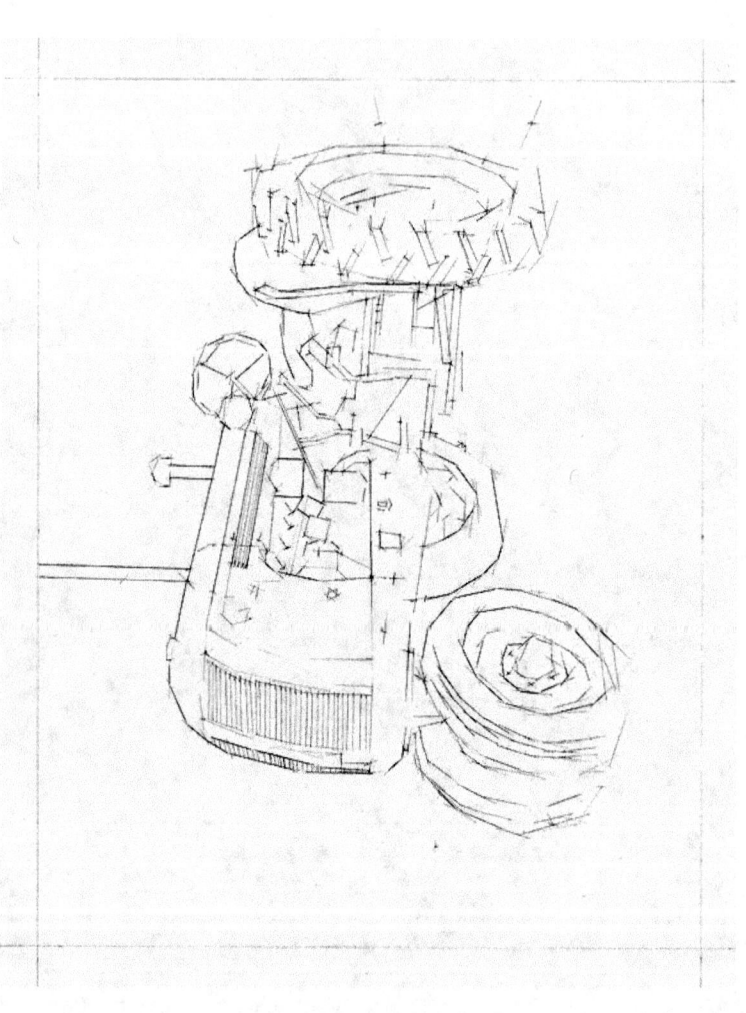

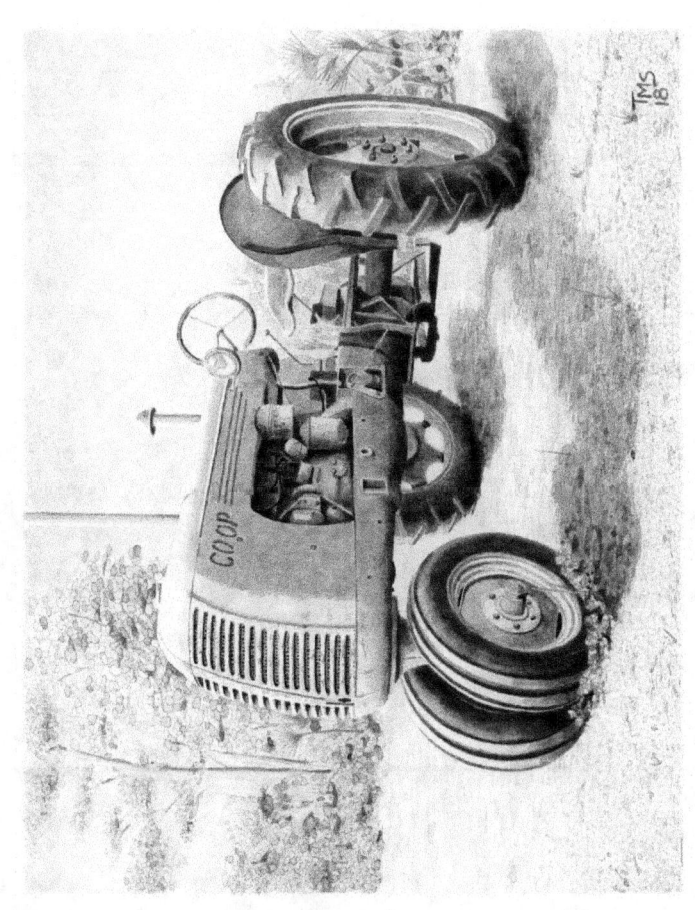

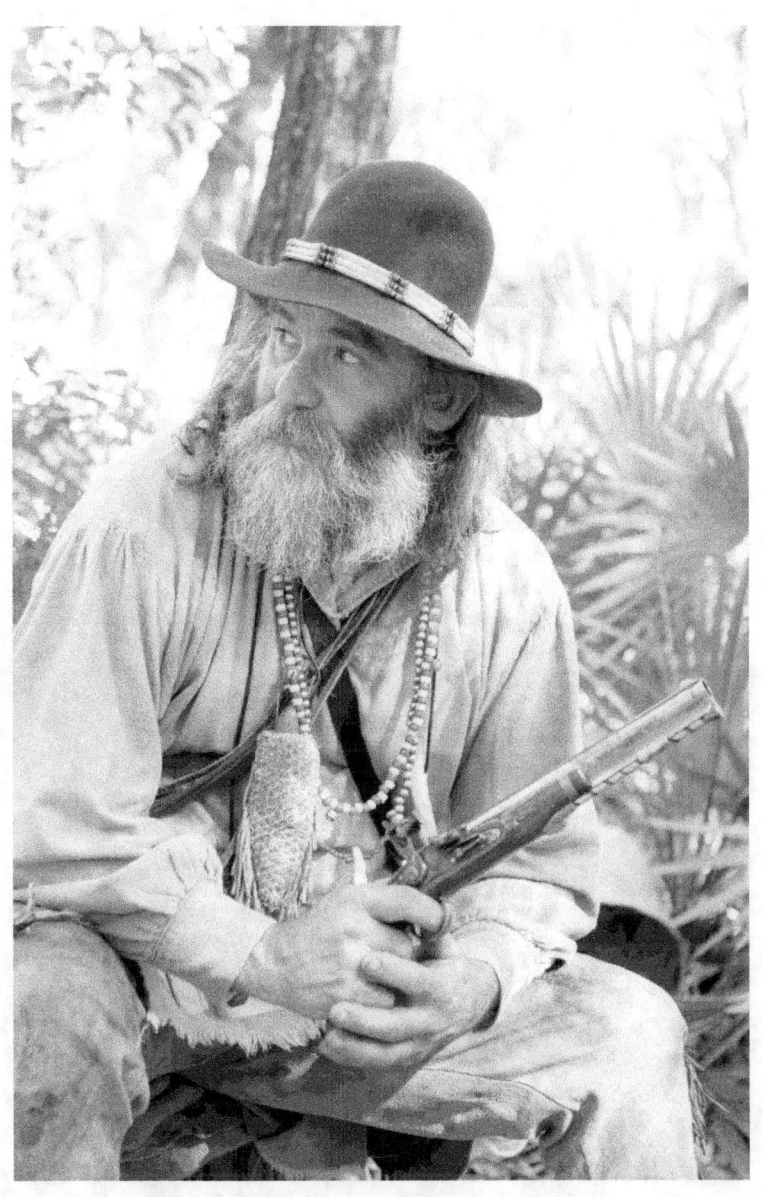

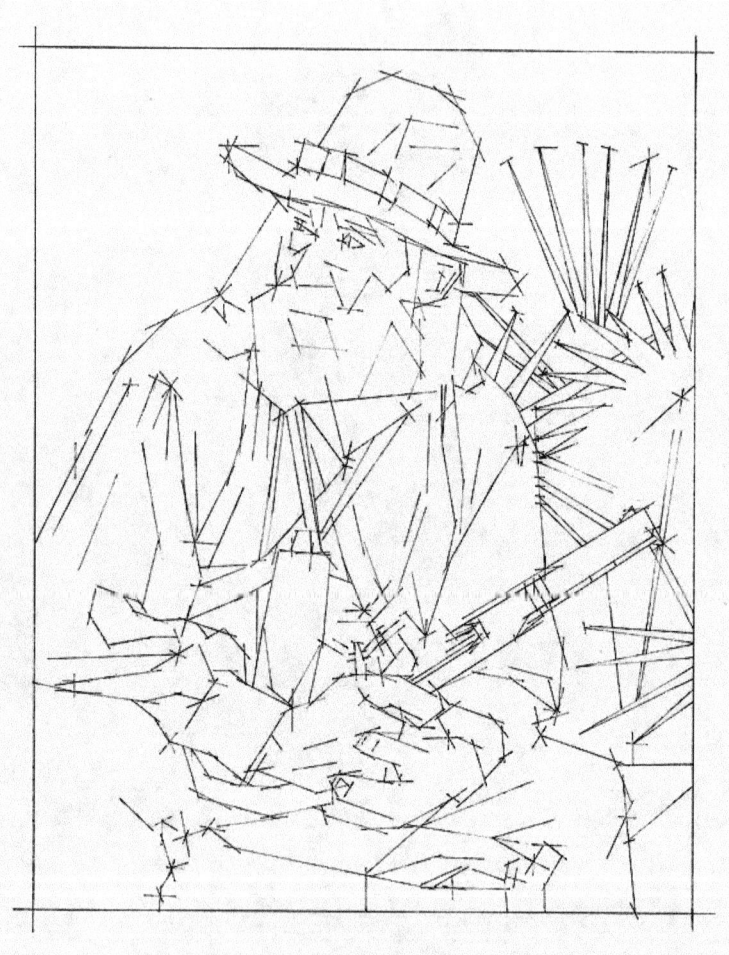

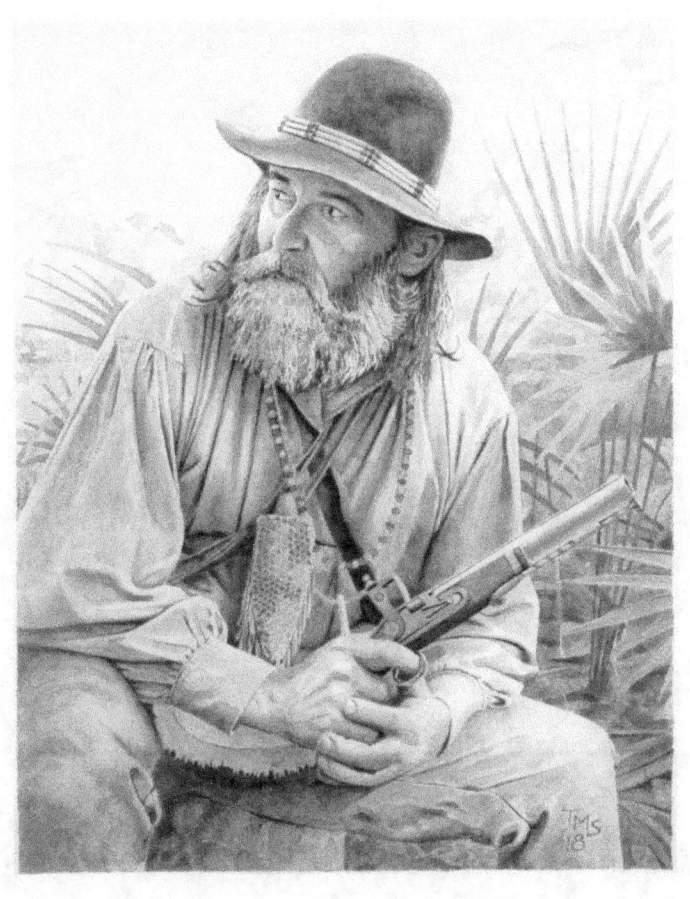

About The Author

Timothy Michaels is a U.S. based artist who paints primarily with coffee, and sometimes with watercolor. He describes his work as realistic fantasy, as he intends for his paintings to be believable as reality, but with subtle adjustments which he hopes makes them better than reality. The angle transfer method is used in creating most of his art.

Tim is a technically-minded, "cerebral thinker" who enjoys science and philosophy. This leads him to constantly analyze his work. While his intent is to improve his art, he also enjoys sharing his discoveries with the art community in book form.

Other Books by Timothy Michaels

"Absolute Relativity: How Newton and Einstein Agree"

"Out of This World: The Movement Dimension"

"The Physics of Color Harmony"

"How We See Art"

"Walking the Cards: A Unique Drawing Method"

His artwork may be viewed at: www.tmsartgallery.com

Readers are invited to comment by sending an email to: 101timsplace@gmail.com

www.ingramcontent.com/pod-product-compliance
Lightning Source LLC
Chambersburg PA
CBHW062351290526
45794CB00005B/2185